May 22, 2014

BJ -

Happy Birthday
for your 31ST I am
giving you a golf manual
for use during your
future long and
satisfying golfing
obsession —

Love Dad -
Mom

Doctor Golf

Doctor Golf

by William Price Fox

Illustrated by
Charles Rodrigues

UNIVERSITY OF SOUTH CAROLINA PRESS

Library of Congress Cataloging in Publication Data

Fox, William Price.
  Doctor Golf.

  Reprint. Originally published: Philadelphia:
Lippincott, 1963.
    1. Golf—Anecdotes, facetiae, satire, etc. 2. Golf
—Fiction. I. Title.
PS3556.097D6 1984   818'.5402   84-10380
ISBN 0-87249-448-9

*The letters in this book are the products of the author's
imagination. Other than those of a few friends, the
names are also fictional.*

Published in Columbia, South Carolina, by
the University of South Carolina Press, 1984

First edition published by
J. B. Lippincott Company, 1963

Manufactured in the United States of America

For Kathy.

Contents

In the hallway at Eagle-Ho, across from the mural of Vardon at Carnoustie and the bust of Tom Morris the Elder, lies the putter of Walter Travis. To the left are the death masks of the great Scots, to the right the glass cases containing shoes, golf gloves, sculptured bronzes of classic grips, autographed balls, and the original leather bag of Bonnie Prince Charlie. And above all this, rising to the great domed ceiling, is the giant bronze plaque with the words of the immortal Henry Leach: "Men who were innocent and have turned to golf do not give a reason why; they are silent to the questioner. They say that he too will see in time, and then they golf exceedingly."

DOCTOR GOLF

Eagle-Ho Sanctuary
Eagle-Ho, Arkansas
October, 1916

1.

Dear Dr. Golf,

You would think that a person who slices would be able to slice only on the golf course. My slice, Dr. Golf, is with me twenty-four hours a day. When I walk I lean to the right, when I stand in an elevator I quickly move to the right side of the car, even when I speak I can see the slice at work, for I now speak out of the right side of my mouth. Lately I have been having splitting headaches in the rightmost portion of my head. All of these things I could tolerate and make allowances for; on the golf course I merely play all shots far to the left side of the fairway. But now something new and ominous is taking place. I have developed a violent tic to the right in my right eye and at the right corner of my mouth, and occasionally the entire right side of my body begins pulsing and burning. The doctors have examined me and find nothing wrong. I have begged and pleaded with them and told them I was positive it was the long-range effect of my slice that has caused this, but they do not listen. . . . Can you be of any help? . . .

> I remain,
> THADDEUS DREHER
> Tupelo, Miss.

Dear Sir,

The phrase "a built-in slice" is not without its physiological basis. The nerve that activates the built-in slice has not been properly isolated and named, but it apparently does not differ too radically from the sciatic nerve. I have handled a score of cases similar to yours and in each case I have had to resort to a combination of hydrotherapy, orgonomy and hypnosis. All treatments were successful. There is very little I can relate in an open letter, but if you are interested in curing this sickness I would be happy to handle your case. All treatments would, of course, be by mail.

As ever,
Dr. Golf

2.

Dear Dr. Golf,

Is there any literature or information available on caddy flogging? I understand it is a recognized part of the game at Eagle-Ho and at all Eagle-Ho clubs.

Bruno Zirato, Jr.
Durham, N. C.

Dear Sir,

Caddy flogging is indeed part of the game here at Eagle-Ho. And a very valuable part of the game, I might add. Once you leave the first tee the code of St. Andrews is in effect. This dates back to 1710 and it clearly states that the caddy has precisely the same rights as any indentured servant.

While the U.S.G.A. has chosen to overrule this practice, we at Eagle-Ho and at all Eagle-Ho clubs still maintain the classic form of caddy flogging as it was during the days of Bonnie Prince Charles. Flogging is done every six holes. This gives the caddy a chance to profit by his mistakes. In all cases of caddy flogging I find the best club to be a soft-shafted midiron. Occasionally I will give my caddy a sharp rap across the shoulders with my driver upon leaving the first tee. This will work wonders for keeping the beggar on his toes. If the caddy is smarting from a previous flogging, I recommend a quick snatching and turning of the bag. If properly done this places the strap across the victim's throat and the desired pressure can be applied by merely rotating the bag to the left. In cases of over- or under-clubbing by the caddy I always administer a severe rap across the shins with the club face. In this admonishment it is, of course, necessary to use the club the caddy selected. The end result here is obvious: (1) the caddy is made aware of his mistake, (2) he will remember the club you strike him with, (3) good sound disciplinarian action is always an excellent idea, and (4) an unpunished caddy will build up a deep resentment often resulting in a com-

plete breakdown of the master-caddy relationship. . . .

Perhaps the best device for caddy training is my Dr. Golf Caddy Breaker. This is a regulation-type leather-lined bag with slots for adding slugs of lead. The particular model I have at this time can handle up to ninety pounds of ballast without upsetting the balance of the bag. I have had rather amazing success with this device, especially with the smaller caddies. The ninety pounds is located near the bottom of the bag and with the added weight of the Dr. Golf Eagle-Ho bag and the full complement of Eagle-Ho woods and irons the caddy's head and shoulders are virtually snapped back. I have always hated to see a caddy slouch and this corrects that odious habit. The Dr. Golf Caddy Breaker also discourages the disgusting tendency in some of the newer clubs of allowing caddies to carry double.

As ever,

Dr. Golf

P.S. Dr. Golf Eagle-Ho Caddy Breaker complete with lead ballast is $196.90 plus postage of $2.40.

3.

Dear Dr. Golf,

Can a ball be moved if it lands in a hole in a sand trap? I am thinking specifically of holes in the sand caused by players playing before you.

Richard Larom

Bayshore, Calif.

Dear Sir,

In answer to your inquiry about moving a ball from a footmark in a sand trap. This is an old ruling, and one I can't put my finger on at the moment. It does state in no uncertain terms that a ball can be removed from a hole caused by a burrowing animal. Hence, we need only apply the simple axiom that since man *is* a burrowing animal, the ball can and should be moved to a smooth portion of the sand.

As ever,
Dr. Golf

4.

Doctor Golf,

I have always carried my clubs face down in my bag with the handles sticking out. Each handle was equipped with a little numbered woolen cover. I used this method because it kept the clubs from rattling and I was also able to keep my opponents confused as to which club I was using. Recently all of the numbered covers were stolen—possibly by my opponents. I carry my own bag. Now I am forced to empty the entire bag of clubs out on the ground before each shot. You can easily see that this makes for a slow round of golf and the extra work is rather considerable. Can you give me some advice.
WILLIAM TURNER
Cold Spring Harbor, N. Y.

Mr. Turner,

You have indeed hit upon something here. It's an excellent idea and one worth pursuing. How often in the heat of tournament play have I wished I could conceal from my opponents what club I was using! But back to your question:

I had to put my thinking cap on for this one, but I believe I have it. First of all, get a much bigger bag. Preferably a large round one. Line the clubs up with the long clubs on the left and short clubs on the right. Now this is it: A closely guarded professional secret is that the midiron is longer than the mashie and the mashie is in turn longer than the mashie niblick and so on. In other words, you have, with a little practice, a built-in code you can follow by merely measuring the club without taking it out of the bag. You merely tell the club by measurement. Under separate cover I have taken the liberty of mailing you one diagram of Doctor Golf's club lengths (suitable for framing) at $2.98 C.O.D., also meter stick $1.98 C.O.D. Since this makes one nice package the postage due will be only $2.40.

As ever,

Dr. Golf

5.

Dear Doctor Golf,

The other day I was talking with my buddy, O. Rooney, and he says, "Mike, how come there are so many Italian golf pros around New York?" What do you say?

Michael O'Shaughnessy
Bronx

Dear Mr. O'Shaughnessy,

How about that! Why, just the other day I was talking to George Fazio* and I asked him the same question. "George," I said, "How come there are so many Italian golf pros around New York?" George is Italian, you know. He says he doesn't know.

As ever,

Dr. Golf

* George Fazio is an Eagle-Ho member.

6.

Dear Doctor Golf,

Nothing, absolutely nothing keeps my head down when I swing. I have tried short tees, no tees, even clubs six inches shorter. I've tried your leaded collar at the back of my neck (up to 19 lbs.); I've even used your steel strapping and cable arrangement No. 97, securing my head and shoulders to the ground, with little or no success. I've been the laughing stock of Early Moravia for nine years with your ingenious but useless apparatus. The last unit was the enormous trifocal-equipped helmet which succeeded only in driving my Doberman pinscher, who is normally a placid dog, absolutely mad.

Doctor Golf, I still have faith in you but, alas, the years are slipping by. Please don't send any more equipment. I'm too weary to unpack the larger units and too jaded and distrustful of the smaller items. Please, Doctor Golf, tell me—shall I give up golf? I have many good years still ahead of me, perhaps fishing, hunting; a friend of mine is a bird watcher. Maybe I should marry and settle down and quit this mad and fruitless pursuit.

I remain, most desperately,

GENE HILL
Early Moravia, N. J.

My dear Mr. Hill,

I know! I know how hard it is! I see by the file of our long correspondence that you are in most serious trouble. Since my devices have not worked, I can now only suggest the terminal method which I reserve for cases such as yours (in extremis).

But, first of all, please ship back C.O.D. the following items: 1. Doctor Golf steel strapping and cable arrangement No. 97; 2. Doctor Golf leaded collar (with weights); 3. Doctor Golf Trifocal Helmet. Since all of these items are guaranteed, you will be given credit on your account upon receipt of the shipment and after inspection.

And now the terminal method. Had you been trying to correct this problem for less than eight years you would not qualify for what I am about to suggest. But nine years with the same problem is a serious problem and I feel it calls for serious measures. Mr. Hill, you are now ready for surgery. I am mailing your file and a covering letter to a practitioner of Doctor Golf Surgery in your part of the country. You will be contacted during the next ten days. He will suggest a suitable date and will work out the necessary details.

One thing more, before you go, eat a good dinner, get plenty of sleep, and bring cash.

As ever,
DR. GOLF

7.

Dear Doctor Golf,

During the past month we have had a caddy uprising here at Canoe Brook. They have banded together into a black leather jacket wearing, knife carrying, scowling, mutinous pack of mercenaries. They roam the fairways and the woods at will in packs of twenty and thirty, attacking members and their guests, insulting women on the greens, destroy-

ing, pillaging, looting, burning. Only God knows
what will happen next. Only God knows where it
will end. As if this were not enough, some of our better members have thrown in with the brigands, and
their voices, too, can be heard in the night, their sil-
houettes seen dancing madly against the great bonfires
on the north course greens. We cannot notify the
authorities, still we cannot submit to this much
longer. Our membership is slipping away, our clubhouse is in shambles, and what few golfers we have
left cautiously venture forth with caddy carts and
rifles. Our professional has been missing for two weeks
and last night his ripped and burned alpaca sweater
was found flying from the flagpole on the third green.

Bob Stuart
Bluefield, W. Va.

Dear Sir,

Since neither you nor your club is Eagle-Ho
there is nothing I can do but point out your folly
for letting these blighters get out of hand.

As ever,
Dr. Golf

8.

Dear Dr. Golf,

In April of this year our club was placed on the
approved list of Eagle-Ho clubs and we inaugurated
caddy flogging. I had grave doubts about this practice at first and I must confess I was fearful. It is
now six months later and after following your books
and manuscripts on the introduction and execution
of caddy flogging we here at Sleepy Knoll, to the
man, are delighted with the results. Our caddies

thrive on this practice, and a new and deep respect for the members has replaced the old indifference of last year.

We were very fortunate in procuring Mr. H. Ashley through your services and we want to say he has truly done a remarkable job. I was very impressed in learning that Mr. Ashley got his background and training handling bird dogs in the Florida Field Trials. Some of the men here believed his insistence on making the caddies "point" balls a trifle inhumane, but when Mr. H. Ashley had these same men question the caddies all doubt of inhumanity was removed. He maintains, and the caddies support his belief, that a caddy's greatest joy is in "pointing" a ball in the classic position. Mr. H. Ashley has even introduced contests to make every caddy familiar with the classic "point" position. And how beautiful it is to watch two youthful caddies springing through the rough and quartering and requartering a field.

Dr. Golf, we have, however, run into one very sensitive problem. Unfortunately, our club is near a highway and motorists and pedestrians can see the caddy stocks Mr. H. Ashley built for flogging. We have had several complaints from the township and the church. Mr. H. Ashley insists that the flogging stations remain in full sight, but our local ministers and teachers are shouting that we must do away with the practice. We were wondering if you could advise us on this subject.

I remain,
RICHARD TROTHINGWELL

Dear Sir,

I am sending you along a copy of Dr. Golf's "Caddies, the Care and Feeding Of." You will please

refer to Chapter 76 entitled "The Floggee-Flogger Relation." This chapter will explain the master-caddy relation as well as the relation between your club and your township. . . .

Mr. Trothingwell, there will always be enemies and narrow-minded people who do not approve of flogging. Why this is, I'm sure I'll never know. But I must insist that as an Eagle-Ho qualified club you do not conceal this practice, that it be done in full view of your club, your wives, your town, indeed your church.

As ever,
Dr. Golf

9.

Dear Doctor Golf,

My opponent is driving me crazy. He will swing at the ball and miss and then claim it was a practice swing. I know he is lying because the veins are standing out in his throat and forehead and he occasionally goes down on one knee from the force of the swing. Question, is there a U.S.G.A. ruling on this?

HARDWICK BLACKSTONE
(UNATTACHED)

Dear Sir,

This is an interesting and, at the same time, very complicated case. It was my pleasure to sit in on the ruling of this procedure. Briefly, it states that the player should be penalized one stroke for missing the ball.

Your case, however, is different. Here you have a clear-cut example of the Baltusrol Ruling. When your opponent goes down on one knee (either knee) you have introduced an entirely different situation. This decision goes back to the St. Andrews ruling of 1919. This clearly states that if a player misses a ball and falls to one knee and shouts Baltusrol, he is not penalized the one stroke. If this is difficult to grasp, it can be compared to a similar ruling in baseball. If the batter misses the third strike and the catcher drops the ball, the batter can run to first providing he gets there before the ball. It's what you might call a little incentive for being on your toes.

But the Baltusrol Ruling is a fair ruling and there is a countermeasure. If the opposing player (in this case, you) suspects that his opponent is going to try for a Baltusrol, he has plenty of time to act. You

merely remove the wood covers from your opponent's clubs. If he then misses, drops to one knee and shouts Baltusrol, you have only to point to the exposed clubs. I find it best to remove the covers while the opponent is addressing the ball. One of the British Opens was lost in this manner not too many years ago. Incidentally, it is the duty of your opponent's caddy to replace the wood covers.

As ever,
DR. GOLF

P.S. I have a nice selection of Doctor Golf wood covers in earth colors, $7.98 per set (4) C.O.D., mailing charge $2.40.

10.

Dear Doctor Golf,

From time to time I hear the phrase "Putter Dwell" mentioned. It is usually associated with your name. Do you have any details on this?

MR. S. RICHARDSON
Princeton, N. J.

Dear Mr. Richardson,

In answer to your question about "Putter Dwell" (this is a copyrighted Doctor Golf term), it would be foolish to attempt to describe this phenomenon in a single letter. There is available a Doctor Golf Eagle-Ho book on this entitled "Putter Dwell (Scientific Basis and Practical Application)." $7.98 C.O.D., $2.40 postage.

"Putter Dwell," or ball drag as the early Scots called it, is that phenomenon of the ball clinging to the putter surface during the split second of impact. An example—albeit absurd, but one which will illustrate this point—is striking the ball with a sponge-faced club. In this case the ball will obviously dwell longer on the sponge than, say, on a chrome-finished face before being propelled forward. Taking the simile one step farther it is easy to see that the longer the putter face stays on the ball the more control one has over it. It must also be added here that an incredibly light touch can be manifested by an application of these principles to the putting stroke.

Given this set of circumstances, how now do we proceed? Obviously a mere dragging of the ball toward the hole with the club is illegal. We must in fact strike the ball with a solid sharp blow with a constantly decreasing club-head speed. Let me summarize this by commenting that on wood shots the club reaches its maximum speed at the moment of impact; in putting, the reverse is true.

Now the problem arises as to how we go about achieving this decreasing club-head speed. How do we arrive at the point of impact with the slowest speed possible and still assure ourselves the ball will be hit firm enough? How do we follow through and take advantage of this new "Putter Dwell" and in effect steer the ball during the now longer moment of impact?

This letter is to clearly point out the complexity of this shot and the necessary knowledge one needs to try it. In fairness, I would say don't try it. Don't try it if you are satisfied with your putting as it now stands. If, however, you are a serious golfer and would like a guaranteed putting average of 32 or less strokes per 18-hole round you should fill out the coupon at the bottom of the page.

Some of the necessary equipment will be the Doctor Golf Eagle-Ho Water-Filled Training Putter, Doctor Golf Eagle-Ho Stone-faced Putter and the now famous Doctor Golf Eagle-Ho Velvet-faced Master's Touch Putter.

As ever,
Dr. Golf

11.

Dear Doctor Golf,

I have just read Mr. Herbert Warren Wind's History of Golf In America. Mr. Wind gives an entire chapter over to discussing Francis Ouimet's victory over Harry Vardon and Ted Ray in the U.S.G.A. Open in 1913 at Brookline. Nowhere in your letters have you ever mentioned Ouimet. Are your feelings so strong and your prejudices so deep against American golfers to allow you this oversight? Surely you recognize the importance of this victory and the tremendous effect it has had on golf in America.

WALTER McQUADE
New York City

Dear Sir,

I, too, have read Mr. Wind's book on golf. For the records I will state that, while I will never approve of Mr. Wind's recognition of all professionals or his adoration of same, I would have to give him a "well done" on his efforts as a chronicler. The bulk of his work is pure and of good quality. Of particular interest and articulation of a most excellent kind, I found his chapter on Vardon, Ray and Ouimet satisfying and superior to anything I have encountered since Bernard Darwin.

As to Ouimet and his victory. I am not made of stone, sir, nor was my Father. We attended Brookline those four wet days in 1913 that shook the golfing world, I as a mere stripling, Father in the full flesh of his manhood. We followed Mr. Harry Vardon all day, every day.

It must be said at this point that since Harry Vardon belonged to Eagle-Ho in Scotland and had spent some time with Father laying out our Glen Eagles course, our support, quite naturally, went with him.

Father could never countenance Ted Ray. He found him too massive and aggressive and he was given to overswinging and chortling in a rather common way with his caddy. As you know the third day ended in a three-way tie—Vardon, Ray, and Ouimet.

During tea that evening Father, myself, and Vardon sat before the fire. Vardon was confident he could defeat Ouimet. Father was fearful that a victory for the caddy would open the game to the public and set golf back a hundred years. He suggested that Vardon carry a quarter whip in his bag and that he occasionally brandish it to remind Ouimet of his proper station in life and the folly of his presumption. Vardon refused this advice and retired early to be ready for the final play-off.

Meanwhile the entire crowd at Brookline, the press, the public, the world, had swung over to Ouimet's side. The facts that the lad had a good swing, was poor, was a caddy, etc., had taken its obvious effect.

The play-off began in earnest at eleven in the morning. Vardon and Ouimet were long off every tee and side by side, while Ted Ray's booming wild woods went crashing through the birch and scuttling into the tall growths and the whins. A goodly crowd of some 4000 souls was present despite the rain, and a splendid match ensued.

On the 14th green Ted Ray's match was over and we perceived that our Harry, who at the time was only one down, was beginning to worry. For young Ouimet was good, he was very good. His shots were as long or longer than Harry's, his irons a bit crisper and his putting authoritative and devastating. On that day in Brookline, Ouimet was unquestionably a better golfer than Vardon.

I am telling you all this to lead up to the historic incident on the 17th green.

It was here that young Ouimet needed one putt from eleven feet to close the match. He studied the downhill, sloping line and then paused. He looked at it again and decided to try and get down in one. And then he glanced at my father. Ouimet must have sensed something. My father smiled at him and held up his thumb and forefinger of his left hand, indicating how the putt would break. My father had capitulated and now was in young Ouimet's camp.

Francis Ouimet then addressed the ball again with the putter blade in front of the ball, then behind it, and struck. The ball held the ridge and the two-inch left line for nine of the eleven feet and then gracefully curved into the very center of the cup. Among the first to cheer was my father and together with Messrs. G. K. Chesterton, John Anderson, and Mungo Park, they hoisted young Ouimet onto their shoulders and carried him to the clubhouse.

There were over 4000 rain-soaked persons cheering that great day at Brookline, but a small portion of that cheer, I will always feel, went to my father who had in one dramatic moment contradicted everything he had ever stood for, who without fear of consequence followed the emotion within him and threw his support to the underdog, the caddy, to the young and gracious Francis Ouimet.

That night I was allowed my first brandy. Father, Harry Vardon, and I sat before the fire. The rain had stopped and it was cold. Sounds of drinking and laughter filled the air but now my father's heart was heavy. I'll never forget his words of that evening for they have proved to be too true. He looked at the fire and spoke to Vardon.

"Harry, the gates are now open and soon the rabble will be in the foothills." He paused for a long while and then added:

"Yes, young Ouimet has prevailed and come spring, the invasion will be upon us."

We drank to the passing of an era, the end of the golden age of golf, and to the single hope in the West—Eagle-Ho.

And then we smashed our glasses on the chestnut log in the leather and brass bound fireplace at Brookline.   As ever,

Dr. Golf

12.

Dear Doctor Golf,

How would you compare the game of today with golf fifty years ago? Were the drivers then as long as today? Were the courses more difficult? I have often wondered if the men of 1905 were given modern equipment would their games have been as good as those today?

EDWARD GREER
Dayton, Ohio

Dear Sir,

The game of today is, it must be admitted, a much more robust and massive one than the one my father and his followers played. The equipment here at Eagle-Ho has not changed dramatically nor, for that matter, have the courses. Other courses have been made easier and in general the modern course does encourage a very vigorous, overpowering game. The excessive width of fairways, the absence of sufficient rough, heather and whins gives the strong man confidence, and long driving is the rule rather than the exception. There were long drivers at the turn of the century, but they were also careful drivers, for a wild drive (and by wild I mean only a few yards left or right off the center of the fairway) was more severely punished by the wilder nature of the roughs and the presence of whins. I am sure if the modern golfers of today were placed at Eagle-Ho now or St. Andrews of 1902 there would be a rapid recalculation upwards of their low and undeserved handicaps.

As ever,
DR. GOLF

13.

Dear Doctor Golf,

Was it your grandfather who on his deathbed spoke the famous word "Fruition," and then passed on?

EUGENE HINMAN
Vassar College
Poughkeepsie

Dear Sir,

You have confused my grandfather with the Reverend Increase Mather of Boston. The word "Fruition" must be accredited to him. My grandfather's last words, however, are a matter of public

record and I would like to pass them on to you and my readers. His death came at the age of 93 in 1896 shortly after the clubhouse at Eagle-Ho was erected and just before the Qualifying Rounds for our first tournament. My father was at his side and he had the last words set down in his chronicle. I quote:

Father raised his baton and beckoned me to him. He was resting easy but I could tell his strength was failing. He had played earlier that morning, but had had trouble with his putts so no final score was posted. I didn't have to bend over, for his voice was still strong. "Son," he said. "Young Chauncey Depew is still having difficulty with his woods. . . . Promise me you'll make him open his stance. Failing that, make him take his club back more slowly. Splendid golfer . . . I'd hate to think of him not qualifying because of that hook." I promised I would. He then smiled, folded his hands and fingers in an interlocking grip around the leather handle, closed his eyes and whispered, "Fore." I have always liked to imagine that he got off a booming drive down the center of No. 7 at Carnoustie or No. 4 at Glen Eagles. Never has a man been better prepared to meet the Great Greenskeeper than father.

Here ends the chronicle.

As ever,
DOCTOR GOLF

14.

Dear Doctor Golf,

I have been having considerable difficulty controlling the speed of my club on my back swing.

Often I will take it back so rapidly that on impact I merely smother the ball. At other times I go back so slow and listless that I lose all control of the grip and the ball might do anything. Is there anything I can use to tell when the proper back-swing speed is being realized?

> JAMES KRIDEL
> New York City

Dear Sir,

I am forwarding to you today four units of my Doctor Golf Eagle-Ho Swing-Speed Whistle Control.

Attach each unit to the top of each of your woods in the manner described on the package. This is a very simple device that I have found very successful. It was patented in 1918 so you can see it has withstood the test of the years.

The device is a carefully pitched whistle which emits a G-sharp note when the club is moving at the proper speed during back swing. If you hear no sound your swing is either too fast or too slow. The whistle has long been a favorite corrective device here at Eagle-Ho. I am sure you will find the results immediately beneficial. Charges are $4.60 for 4 units plus $2.60 postage.

As ever,
DOCTOR GOLF

15.

Dear Doctor Golf,

While I have never qualified for Eagle-Ho Sanctuary privileges I have long been a member of the International Eagle-Ho club. I am 46 years of age, in robust health, and enjoy a handicap of 2. I now feel the time has come for me to marry. I have, I'm sure you will be pleased to know, decided to sire a line of golfers who will follow in my footsteps. I have often thought that had I begun my golf career at an earlier age, instead of at 30, I would now be at Eagle-Ho. The sons I raise will be Eagle-Ho oriented from the day they are able to walk.

At this time I have no fiancée. Before running an advertisement and seeking out a candidate, I was wondering if you have any thoughts on selecting a woman capable of producing good golf stock.

Yours very truly,
JOHN D. MACDONALD
Pond Creek, Okla.

Dear Sir,

In the fall of this year I am publishing a book entitled "On the Care and Selection of a Wife." The book is mainly directed at an examination of handicaps before and after marriage and a correlation showing the type of woman that can be identified with a low handicap player.

There is also a long chapter on the selection of a wife for the purposes you describe; namely, breeding golfers. Since your problem is so acute, I will send you galley proofs of this book as soon as they are available. In the meantime I will list a number of points that you can keep in mind during your initial investigations. In the book, each of these items is expanded:

1. Avoid women of delicate fibre and weak digestion.

2. Avoid smallish women. Small women tend toward nervousness, headaches, shortness of breath, and general irritability. A full-sized, generous, or even large woman is always preferable.

3. Shun small-boned women. A woman of thin ankles and wrists will produce children with the same tendency. A delicate-boned man has little chance of ever developing his game beyond the cautious, middling, weak-drive variety. As a consequence, and especially on long courses, he will find it impossible to break 80. A thin waist in a woman can only mean inner distortion, eventual pain in birth, and thin boned and framed children. Search out, then, a woman with a moderate or thick waist, ankles and wrists, and of a more comfortable size. This type, the short, powerful type, produces the golfers of tomorrow.

4. Avoid women with dropsy or those given to melancholia.

5. Search out a woman of clear eyes. Beware of myopia, astigmatism. Avoid shortness of breath. (Repeat.)

6. If possible, search out good Scottish, Welsh, or Nordic stock. Avoid French unless from northern latitudes. In no case marry Mediterranean or Macedonian types.

7. A talkative mate must be shunned. Beware of sharp-tongued babblers schooled in current events, politics, or Aristotelian logic.

8. Avoid women who believe in entertaining at home.

9. Avoid being misled through extravagance of ornament or coiffure of hair. A rule to follow is that her inward life, which is also that part of her life which she will pass on to your sons, can be determined by her outward form. A highly decorated woman means a low organic quality of the brain and

it will produce sluggish, feeble and inferior children.

Study the birds in the air. Does not the male bird have the bright feathers, the ornamental plumage, while the hen's raiments and colors are confined to the browns and buffs that best camouflage her in the nest? Choose, then, a mate who is best suited to the nest. Look not for the flashy or the fleshless, but to one who will keep the house and the children in a state that will do you proud in your community. Choose then a gentle woman, a strong, silent woman and one who is grateful for the respect and trust you are bestowing upon her.

> As ever,
> DOCTOR GOLF

16.

Dear Doctor Golf,

> *How does your library at Eagle-Ho compare to the U.S.G.A.'s in New York City?*
>> GEORGE EVANS
>> *Palo Alto, Calif.*

Dear Sir,

Occasionally I am very harsh on U.S.G.A. policies and the commercialization that has permeated their once-glorious ranks. But someone, I feel, must be the standard bearer, and my obligation to Eagle-Ho and the Code of St. Andrews will not let me tolerate their many defections.

While the U.S.G.A. has been lax in many areas, they have persevered and done admirably in equipping and maintaining their library in New York. The collection of books and trophies is of wide range and of good quality. Their brownstone is in good repair, and the atmosphere of history pervades the quiet and dignified reading rooms.

Their research material, scholarly papers, and genealogical tables are not so complete or of the excellence as are ours at Eagle-Ho. I feel I can state without fear of successful contradiction that, while the U.S.G.A. library at New York can no more be compared to ours than it can to the first-millennium one that stood at Alexandria, it is an excellent—if modest—establishment that the golfers of New York can well be proud of.

As ever,
Doctor Golf

17.

Dear Doctor Golf,

I have a handicap of four. My fiancée has a handicap of twelve. We enjoy playing together and team well in the Blind Bogey and Mixed Foursome tournaments. We have won many prizes and are, in short, very much in love. In August, following the First Qualifying Round of the Governor's Cup, we plan to marry.

I have a question and a request.

The question: Do you think the difference in handicap (8) will work any hardship on our marriage? The request: We would like to fly out to Eagle-Ho and have you marry us. If this cannot be arranged, we would appreciate some official document from Eagle-Ho with your blessings.

Very truly yours,
Mr. John D. MacDonald
Sarasota, Fla.

P.S. I have followed all of your advice in your letter to me in October.

Dear Sir,

Surely you know that I have never, nor will I ever, recognize any woman golfer. In all likelihood this young lady's true handicap is more like twenty than twelve, and after you marry it will probably soar to forty. The years will compound the difference in handicap of eight to thirty, and I can foresee only misery. Heavy food, whelping of children, and sloth will produce a shortened swing, a too forceful right hand, and an uncorrectable diving hook in your mate.

You, sir, will progress from lack of proper sleep, through improper stool, to hypertension and melancholia; and to find the peace you are now so willing to throw away you will have to develop a slashing slice to free yourself from the fetters of walking down the fairway with what now is your soul mate. There is no sadder sight than seeing a couple whom folly has joined together being separated by the passing of the years.

I cannot give you my blessings. I can only warn you and implore you to think this over very carefully. I would suggest that you play a few rounds alone, possibly on a strange course, and try to envision what misery lies ahead for you in the years to come. While others are playing abroad and entertaining possible ideas of Eagle-Ho, you, sir, will be playing fewer and flatter holes with your heavy hammed and hocked life mate. It would be better if you had the gout than to make this foolish and irretrievable move. A Russian whose name escapes me once wrote to a Macedonian golfer that a golf marriage, such as this lamentable thing you describe, "can be likened to a man plunging his hand into a box of snakes hoping to draw forth an eel."

As ever,
DOCTOR GOLF

18.

Dear Doctor Golf,

I am doing my doctorate here at Harvard on Early Nineteenth Century Golf with special emphasis on the iron clubs. To acquaint you with my work I have a complete history with a full bibliography of your grandfather's split with St. Andrews in 1880. In my oral dissertation I defended his position before three golf scholars and was awarded a purple and white sash. I also have woodcuts showing the first Eagle-Ho clubhouse on the grounds of what now is Glen Eagles.

My problem is as follows: I have records from 1770 to 1890 on descriptions of iron clubs. Unfortunately, one letter is missing. The letter I am referring to is from a Mr. Miles Bantock and it was sent to your father sometime around 1888. I believe your father answered it that same year. In particular, the letter describes the original iron used by Duncan Forbes of Culloden and Prince Charles. Most of the records of this period (1880–1890) were lost in a conflagration at Edinburgh in 1909. Your father's letter, if it is extant, is the only remaining testimony describing this rare club. It is absolutely essential that I have a copy of this letter and if you can obtain it for me I would be eternally grateful.

GEORGE WHEELHORSE
Cambridge, Mass.

Dear Sir,

I have read several of your papers and am pleased with your work. I have also studied Mr. Miles Bantock's letters and papers at some length. We have a book here at Eagle-Ho by him entitled "On Many

Greens" which I am sure you are aware of. Mr. Bantock's talents were slight and most of his work centered around semihumorous stories and a rather tepid form of badly designed Alexandrian verse. His book has no bibliography, which I'm sure will affront your scholarly inclinations, and his random quotations confuse more often than illumine.

However, I do have the letter you are looking for. Mr. Bantock did write my father a question. In Mr. Bantock's fashion the question was rhetorical and he answered it on the same page. If the libraries at Edinburgh and St. Andrews are under the impression that my father answered this letter I would appreciate your setting this matter straight.

The letter bears the date of April 6, 1899. I quote:

Roughly speaking, just as our wooden clubs, drivers, and brassy are heavier, more inelegant, and more powerful than those of Duncan Forbes of Culloden and Prince Charlie, so our iron clubs are lighter, less inelegant, and more varied. The old iron club was probably used nowhere but in whins, in sand, in roads, and other hazards. It was of prodigious size and weighted like a Lochaber ax or other deadly weapon. If it was lighter it was very concave, and had queer sharp tusks. Examples may be seen in the ancient clubs at St. Andrews and at Wimbledon.

Here the chronicle is illegible. A paragraph later he continues with some rather common knowledge on balls. I quote:

As to balls, the old leather stuffed with feathers was as good as the modern gutta-percha while it was fresh and uninjured. Oddly enough, they flew better when they were accidentally cut by iron strokes and around 1850 when mankind first notched them with the sharp end of a ham-

mer and then cast them in notched moulds, as
at present.

I hope this information is satisfactory and if I
find additional material I shall send it forward forth-
with. Incidentally if ever those woodcuts of Eagle-Ho
are placed up for sale I would appreciate your con-
tacting me first.

As ever,
DOCTOR GOLF

19.

Dear Doctor Golf,

Recently I read a book of golf jokes with marvelous illustrations by Fairfax Johnson.

One joke in particular struck me as very funny
and I must pass it on to you. . . . Two golfers, soak-
ing wet, are leaning into a heavy rain. There is lightning flashing. The host says to the guest, "This next
hole No. 11 takes us right past the clubhouse." The
other golfer, the guest, is very dour, having had what
appears to be a very bad game, replies, "It's not going
to take me past."

Yours very truly,
WILLIAM CONCORD
Green Pond, N. C.

Dear Sir,

Precisely why do you feel you must pass on this
form of humor to me? I have little enough time as
it is to answer the serious letters of my members and
friends without having my desk cluttered up with this
folderol. In future kindly spare me this humor and
save it for the public baths.

As ever,
DOCTOR GOLF

20.

Dear Doctor Golf,

Would you please describe your famous but seldom discussed flag shot. I intend trying it out.

J. McDermott
Westport, Conn.

Dear Sir,

I do not recommend this shot to any but the most expert. It takes an incredible amount of practice, dexterity, skill and knowledge, and must be executed with an authority and dash unlike any other golf shot. The slightest miscalculation can spell ruin and what could have been one or two strokes can easily become four, five, or more.

Briefly explained the flag shot is as follows:

No. 1. The shot can not be executed from less than five yards or more than twenty yards from the edge of the green. In the event the green is unusually long, a rule of thumb would be never to attempt a shot of more than forty yards.

No. 2. The wind must be blowing at a right angle of 90 degrees, plus or minus 10 degrees to the flight of the ball toward the pole and traversing the area at a speed of not less than five knots or more than nine. This wind speed can be determined by casting one gram of dry sunflower seeds from a height of five feet onto a flat portion of the green or a close-cropped part of the apron. The seeds should fall in a pattern of not less than three feet in diameter or not more than six feet.

No. 3. The cloth of the flag must be free from excessive dirt and should be of a good quality canvas.

No. 4. A dry day is preferable to a moist day. A sling psychrometer reading of a relative humidity of 40–30 is excellent, 50–40 good, 60–50 fair, 70–60 dubious, 70 and above unsatisfactory.

No. 5. The ball must be struck with a sharp downward rap. Little or no follow-through is needed, for the desired effect is a tight, pinched shot with maximum backspin imparted.

Assuming all these factors are in order, the utmost concentration is then required. The ball is aimed and struck for an area on the flag two thirds and no more than three fourths toward the post from the trailing edge. As to the vertical axis, dead center is excellent but three inches up or below is satisfactory depending on moisture, speed of ball, and the amount of backspin. If all this works, what follows is a most beautiful result. The ball folds the waving flag in upon itself, a brief moment elapses and then the ball is discharged. Often it falls directly into the hole; always it falls no more than three or four inches from the hole. Again let me caution you that this is a most hazardous shot, since the desired speed of flight is great and any miscalculation will plunge the ball deep into the woods or the circling gallery.

However, once this shot is mastered and you turn this magnificent weapon to bear on an opponent you will rapidly dissolve any hopes he may have of defeating you.

I would be interested in hearing from you again after you have experimented with this shot.

As ever,
Dr. Golf

21.

Dear Doctor Golf,

In your letter to me of May 6th describing the flag shot you failed to mention the recommended club. I have experimented for several weeks with the nine-iron and wedge with little or no luck. I have also tried the two-iron. So far I can only report that the portion of the flag you describe is a very small target and I am having immense difficulty striking it.

J. McDermott
Westport, Conn.

Dear Mr. McDermott,

Let me apologize for this gross oversight. I was so pleased and enthusiastic with the prospect of someone not in Eagle-Ho attempting my flag shot that I was carried away and simply forgot to mention the club.

Mr. McDermott, I like your spirit and am delighted with your progress. I can only add, keep trying, keep trying. For while the road may be rough and discouraging, the rewards are incalculable. Mr. McDermott, I would like to know more about you. Yours is the type I encourage to visit Eagle-Ho. If you are interested I would be glad to send along applications and the necessary forms. Who knows, perhaps there is a place here for you.

As to the proper club, the niblick or the midiron will never do. They are probably the reason you are having so much initial trouble. The club I recommend, and the only club that will meet all the requirements of this demanding shot, is the Baffy-Spoon. I have a small supply available at $36.70 each plus $2.60 postage. I will also enclose a photograph of myself demonstrating this great but rather un-popular shot.

As ever,
DR. GOLF

22.

Dear Doctor Golf,

My husband is a follower of your Eagle-Ho form of golf. He takes little or no interest in me, his children, or his home. He gets off the commuter train at Ardsley at 5:20 and instead of coming home he goes directly to the first tee at the Country Club. Upon finishing nine or eighteen holes, depending on the season of the year, he showers at the club and comes home. During winter months he leaves work two hours early and tees off at 3:30 to avoid playing in the dark.

When he arrives home he is nervous and irritable and finds fault with everything I do to make him a nice home. He cannot stand the children and will only visit them when they are asleep. You would think that a round of golf each day plus all day on Saturday and Sunday would be enough, but apparently it is only enough to whet his insatiable appetite.

During our late dinner he reads from Eagle-Ho texts and periodicals, often aloud. After dinner he polishes, waxes and caresses his clubs before the fire and has brandy with them. Lately he is having a slump in putting and he will rise in the middle of the night and tap balls across the bedroom rug toward the night light.

Doctor Golf, I am used to his late arrival, the fatherless children, his complete avoidance of any-thing domestic, and the steady tap-tap-tapping far into the early morning; but lately I have a new and deeper fear and one in which I hope you will offer some help. Last week my oldest boy, Robin, age 6, picked up a putter-stick and began putting the balls with his father. At first I thought my husband would harm the boy, for a weird and strange light came into his eyes. It developed that my husband now thinks the boy has natural talent and he has set out a program to develop his game. His first move was to take the boy out of school. They ride to his office in the morning and there, I am told, lock the office door and putt all day.

I'll not go on; the rest by now must be obvious. I am in desperate need of help. I have reconciled myself to the life of living with this man, but the thought of losing the boy in the same manner frightens me.

I realize I have painted a rather dark picture of my life with my husband; perhaps I have not been altogether truthful. Often we have whole days and week ends together. During the rainy days in February he stays home. During Hurricanes Carol and Edna we passed many happy hours together and he explained the true significance of Eagle-Ho. A wet season, however, is my only hope of seeing him with his children and then the wetness must be of an extreme quality. No ordinary rain or threat of lightning will keep him home, but when the hurricanes strike and the cold rains of February come I make the most of our brief encounters and find the happiness I need to sustain me throughout the long season. My only problem and fear is for the boy.

Mrs. M. Wilkinson
Scarsdale, N. Y.

P.S. My husband's handicap has been 11 for seventeen years.

Dear Mrs. Wilkinson,

There should be more women like you. I have often proclaimed that behind every good golfer stands a great woman. A woman given to long silences and a stately, steady, abiding love uncluttered by the frivolous ideas of togetherness and other trite and absurd philosophies. How fortunate Mr. Wilkinson is to have married such a splendid, understanding woman. Again let me express my respect and admiration to you and the most gratifying life you are surely living.

As to the boy, I believe your apprehensions are too accelerated. The years change not only handicaps but ambitions. Soon this lad will be in college, he will be among the friends he will make for life. Here the battle will be waged for his interest, his vocation, his calling.

I would like a more detailed account of the lad's progress in golf, but I would like for you to wait at least six months before setting this information down. If by the age of seven he shows an indication toward an upright swing and is able to impart wrist action in his middle-iron game, I would be interested in seeing movies of his game. At that time we will decide what should be the proper course his life should follow.

Mrs. Wilkinson, talent—true talent—in golf is one of the brightest stars in the constellation and if it can be discovered before the age of eight what a magnificent thing it can become.

As ever,

DR. GOLF

P.S. The club you referred to as putter-stick is incorrect. The correct word is putter.

23.

Dear Doctor Golf,

I understand that James II in 1681 played a match in Edinburgh teamed with a golfing cobbler, John Paterson, against two British noblemen. The stake was very high and when James and the cobbler won, James gave half the wager to John Paterson to build a golf clubhouse at 77 Canongate, Edinburgh.

Based on the available records I can only surmise that John Paterson was the first golf professional and that the house James II had him build was the first clubhouse. Would you care to comment on this?

HARRISON BERKELEY
Denver, Colo.

Dear Sir,

First let me caution you on the proper use of any, and all, bibliography. While your information on James II and John Paterson is correct, I would advise against using the phrase "I understand," for in truth, sir, you do not since you chose to copy almost word for word this rather common knowledge from the eleventh edition of the Encyclopaedia Britannica. It was my pleasure to have worked on this article with Mr. Horatio Gordon Hutchinson and I find cribbing of your sort beneath contempt.

As for your question about John Paterson, there are genealogical reports and ships' logbooks available that clearly state he returned to cobbling. Eventually his family emigrated to this country and settled in the Midwest. I would imagine they saw the presumption of their grandfather playing with James II and have continued on with cobbling or some adjacent vocation.

As ever,
DR. GOLF

24.

Dear Doctor Golf,

Often I get tired of reading just Eagle-Ho material. I find I get to a saturation point and am in desperate need of some other reading during the long winters. Would it be presumptuous to ask if you have a recommended reading list to ease me through the long winter periods.

OLAF THORGERSEN
Thule, Greenland

Dear Sir,

A few of the books I find rewarding and relaxing might be of help to you. Before listing these I would like to call your attention to a book I am having published this summer which should help you in your problem. The book is my "Doctor Golf Anthology of Verse and Stories." It is a 2000-page leather-bound and boxed edition of the verse and stories I have been gathering since 1930.

As for the list, a brief start would be:

GREEK

Aeschylus, Socrates, Euripides—I would suggest all of these, with emphasis on the Orestean cycle. Do not go further than Euripides, for Aristophanes and his followers are too zesty and filled with smut.

ROMAN

Virgil here. The others, with the possible exception of Catullus, when they are not copying the Greeks and the Manichaeans, are mainly concerned with reporting scandals and various other keyhole-type dirt, i.e., Procopius. Tacitus's *Germania* is excellent and it often unknowingly evokes a spirit of golf.

GERMAN

Of the Germans, I can only recommend Walther von der Vogelweide. After him the Germans became interested in death, Freud, and the Categorical Imperative.

FRENCH

Here I recommend nothing. The French encourage sloth, salons, and a generally feminine society.

All of Dostoevsky. None of Tolstoi or Chekov. Tolstoi is a matter of private conviction. If Tolstoi were alive I am sure we would be archenemies over the question of public golf. In Tolstoi's later life he came around to the absurd belief in the equality of man. Dostoevsky never entertained such excesses. As for Chekov, the man is a hopeless incompetent with virtually nothing to say.

ENGLISH

Kipling, David Hume, Malthus, John Locke, Marlowe, Kenneth Grahame; Wodehouse, possibly Shakespeare.

AMERICAN

Since the death of Michael Wigglesworth no American has come to the literary front worth mentioning. If it is at all possible, please refrain from any and all American writers.

If you have any questions or would like this list supplemented let me know.

As ever,
DR. GOLF

25.

Dear Doctor Golf,

In the spring, as per our recent letters, I am coming to Eagle-Ho. I cannot tell you how overjoyed I am at this time. I have sold my home and properties and have but a few more details to clear up before departing.

In keeping with your policy of not allowing members to bring excessive personal effects along, I have disposed of everything I own except my record library. As you know, I have a rather large record library and I find I am having considerable difficulty in parting with some of the Landowska harpsichord recitals and many of the Beethoven Quartets. You have assured me several times that all the records I have listed are in your music room and are available at all times to Eagle-Ho members, but I still cannot bring myself to dispose of the elder Scarlatti, the Bach Inventions and Chorales, and my complete sets of Monteverdi and Palestrina. I am eager to depart for Eagle-Ho, but my heart is torn on this problem. Could I not get a special waiver and bring along just the Landowska and the Scarlatti?

Very truly yours,
Oscar Berlin
Mt. Holly, N. J.

Dear Sir,

How well I know what anguish you are undergoing and how foolish it now appears I have been to insist that you sell your complete collection. While you can be assured we have all the records you listed last month plus, what I'm sure you will soon admit, some excellent madrigals, Basque rondos, and possibly the finest assortment of Bach and Beethoven in the country, I am granting you a special dispensation and am allowing you to bring any or all of your library. Over the years I have discovered that men who truly appreciate the artistry of the harpsichord and Beethoven's Quartets invariably make sound putters and have little trouble around the green. There appears to be a very sound correlation between classical music lovers and classical golfers.

We are looking forward to seeing you.

As ever,
Dr. Golf

P.S. If you could possibly arrange to lay your hands

on one of the earlier Florence Foster Jenkins recordings I will be grateful. I would love to have her "Bell Song" from *Lakmé*. I believe the accompanist was one Cosmo McMoon.

D.G.

26.

Dear Doctor Golf,

I have read over and over again that the action of the wrists at impact can be compared to striking a blow with a hammer or flinging back a typewriter carriage. I have purchased several hammers as well as a typewriter and I have tried to simulate this effect with no success. While I have good strong hands and wear a Brooks Brothers Size 8 glove, I still cannot bring them into my shots with any feeling of power.

JONATHAN CASO
White Plains, N. Y.

Dear Sir,

Your problem is the same as hundreds of gentlemen golfers of your station in life. Most of the rubbish written for the papers and the magazines of today compare wrist action to activities in life that few golfing men have experienced. In other words, if they instructed you to hold a baffy-spoon in the same manner as a Welsh entrenching tool you would be, and justifiably so, at a loss.

Search not yourself in this fault, for it is not yours but lies among the clerks and sellers of pork who write these dismal instructions. Had you read Eagle-Ho techniques earlier there would now be no question.

I liken the hand action at impact to that of striking a manservant, applying a quarter whip to a caddy, or lashing a stallion over a brook during the heat of the chase. Any of these actions should immediately conjure up the delay in wrist action, the explosive acceleration, and the smooth and finished follow-through. I trust this information will be of assistance.

As ever,
DR. GOLF

27.

Dear Doctor Golf,

I am 36 years old and right-handed. At the top of my back swing I have a problem. I relax my little finger and the finger next to it of my left hand. I believe this is called "playing the piccolo." This relaxation of my left hand allows my right hand to dominate the shot and causes a vicious hook.

I have taken hundreds of hours of lessons, have tried strapping my fingers to the shaft, have swung cross-handed, and have even experimented with two metal hoops placed so I can insert the fingers and weld them to the grip. Despite all this, and more, nothing works and I continue to hook my irons and hood my woods and score in the high eighties. What can I do?

FRANK HEMPHILL
Columbia, S. C.

Dear Sir,

This is one of the most difficult problems to correct in golf. On the surface it sounds easy, but the psychological effort required in securing these fugitive fingers can be, and often is, shattering. Many golfers are guilty of this malfunction in grip and it usually results in the game you describe.

Apart from a sheer act of will to correct this there are several other methods involving varying degrees of difficulty.

1. Allow fingers to float off the grip during your address. Keep the two fingers free of the grip during take-away and back swing. At top of swing bring two fingers in gently and then increase pressure as downswing acceleration begins. This often works with a modicum of practice. Failing this, I would suggest:

2. A piece of No. 4 sandpaper glued to area where "fugitive fingers" fit often makes one more conscious of loosening grip.

3. A fast-setting adhesive or glue. (Do not use epoxy resins.) This is excellent, but removal of fingers from handle can be painful if proper solvent (ethyl alcohol) is not available. Excessive use of solvents can cause skin damage so this method is to be used on a restricted basis.

4. Hypnosis with a proper control has been tried in many instances with more than moderate success. I have used hypnosis for other problems. Often the patient is cured, but a listless quality invades the personage and the long game is greatly reduced.

5. If all these remedies fail, there are two more of a more permanent nature that I will touch upon. A high-pressure cylinder of methyl ethyl ketone if carried in the bag and used every three holes can freeze the fingers to the shaft. While the tissue damage is slight, it is of a cumulative nature caused by the constant freezing and defrosting of said members of the hand. There is also the problem of slowing play to allow freezing and setting of fingers on the various clubs. In the event you try this it would be

advisable to have all handles lathed down to same size.

6. The final remedy, and one which I do not recommend unless all hope is gone, is called "Digitalis Rigis." Before undertaking this I would suggest you speak to someone in Eagle-Ho in your state. I would prefer to let him make the decisions after hearing your particular case. It is a quick and rather painless operation, but the consequences cannot always be determined unless all the facts are known and your history and ambitions are carefully considered.

As ever
DR. GOLF

28.

Dear Doctor Golf,

Last month we had a rather nasty experience here at our club. One of our low handicappers, who shall be nameless, came onto the 18th tee 3 under par. It was to have been his greatest round, and a number of members hurried out from the clubhouse to cheer him in. Unfortunately he pushed two balls out of bounds, shanked a third and wound up with an 11 and a final medal score of 77. Apparently the tension was too great for him. The member returned to the locker room and securing a short piece of rope hanged himself in the bootblack's closet. We have managed to avoid any scandal.

The question I would like to pose is, Why does excessive pressure tend to produce a pushed or sliced shot.

C. CONNELL
New York City

Dear Sir,

Often a golfer who is under the emotional strain of scoring a low medal round will fail to hit the ball as sharply as needed. He tends to play the shot "cozy," which produces a half swing or an unfinished follow-through. There is also a tendency to soften up the right-hand action at impact, which also contributes to a slice or pushed shot.

I am sorry you didn't contact me earlier as I would have advised a bolder, more courageous game for this chap and I'm sure we would have avoided this incident. What was his handicap? Had he had any eagles?

As ever,
DR. GOLF

29.

Dear Doctor Golf,

Last month I passed the final qualifications for Eagle-Ho membership. I am now in the midst of getting my things in order and should be leaving for the Sanctuary in the next fortnight. I was wondering if you have any provisions for fall-out shelters at Eagle-Ho.

RICHARD TRIPPE
Atlanta, Ga.

Dear Sir,

Last year we had two grave problems here at Eagle-Ho. The first, and of the greater magnitude, concerned the excessive crab-grass accumulation near the aprons of the 16th and 18th greens. The second was the decision on fall-out.

Late in the summer we solved the crab-grass problem by using one of the fertilizer salt cures handed down to us by Tom Morris. Following this, I then tackled the problem of shelters.

At first I thought it would be wise to equip one of the salt caves that run under the Mungo Park series of bunkers on the 11th hole. These caves have their own underground springs and, owing to their great depth, they could, with a little construction, serve as a princely shelter. I had convinced myself that this was the plan to follow, and I was on the verge of instructing my masons and carpenters to begin work when another thought assailed me.

It was then that I imagined my friends and my members sitting in an underground cave under their beloved Eagle-Ho and I was saddened. My decision then sprang full-blown from the question: In the absence of golf, what is there left? Without further deliberation I seized my quill and wrote out, and issued that same day, my Edict on Fall-Out Shelters.

Briefly stated, it reads that radioactive fall-out is not recognized. Absolutely no provision will be made, no shelters constructed, and no warning devices, literature, or first aid will be made available.

In the unlikely event that fall-out comes, and I strenuously assure you it won't, what better place, what richer time would one want to go than on the crab grass free, dappled and waving Bermuda of one of the world's finest courses.

As ever,
DR. GOLF

30.

Dear Dr. Golf,

A magazine has assigned me to do a profile of you and Eagle-Ho for the fall issue. The piece could run 30 pages or so. I am sure you can see how much work we have in front of us. It is imperative that I get as much information as possible within the next week in order to present an outline to the editors by next month.

I plan to stop over in Arkansas on my way to the Coast (where I'm profiling Steve McQueen, Joey Dee, and Paul Anka before jetting on to Japan to see my tailor and do a piece on the Nip Twist joints). I will grab a Hertz car and drop by Eagle-Ho around four o'clock Friday.

Don't go to any trouble about food as I'm an old potluck man from way back. I'd appreciate your making arrangements for me for the night.

Looking forward to meeting you, I remain,
NORTON PLUNKETT

P.S. Had lunch at Toots' new spot. He and Jackie Gleason say hello.

Dear Sir,

    If you are capable of doing a profile of me from 700 yards, which is the distance from the gate at Eagle-Ho to my chambers, Godspeed.

DOCTOR GOLF

31.

Doctor Golf,

Every January out here at Pebble Beach I have a little tournament which may have escaped your attention. It's nothing like the Masters or the Open, but we get good TV coverage, have a lot of laughs, and once in a while someone turns in a good score card. Our main attraction is the pro celebrity. This year, I'd like to invite you as my professional guest. If you can fit the round in with your schedule I can arrange a match for us with Sam Snead and Phil Harris.   I remain,

           BING CROSBY

Dear Sir,
     Who are you?

           DOCTOR GOLF

32.

Dear Doctor Golf,

In a recent picture of you at the 18th hole at St. Andrews you are speaking to a man that I could have sworn was Judge Crater. Could this be?

           J. W. KIPLINGER
           New Smyrna Beach, Fla.

Dear Sir,

In the picture you are referring to, the man is Mr. Henry Jordan. There is a resemblance, and a striking one at that. Perhaps they are related.

Shortly after this photograph was taken, I took young Jordan aside and accepted him into Eagle-Ho. He now fully realizes the folly of his past actions and the incalculable harm he has brought to golf in bringing it to the public and elevating the position of the P.G.A.

Jordan's prowess with short irons, despite his wide stance, and his full recantation of his statements encouraging the public golfer made him eligible for Eagle-Ho membership last year. The probational year had just ended and I met Henry at this St. Andrews match. During brandy after dinner that evening young Jordan made a splendid speech to the members, stating that admission to Eagle-Ho, to him, was an even greater triumph than his win at Wentworth in 1922.

As ever,
DR. GOLF

33.

Dear Doctor Golf,

Is there such a shot as a "hosel shot"? My friends here at the Snapping Shoals Country Club say there is and that you are the one who invented it.

FLEETWOOD MOKE
Snapping Shoals, Ga.

Dear Sir,

Someone is pulling your leg, sir. While their humor is of an excellent quality, and I applaud it vigorously, their knowledge of golf is scant, for this is a shot that can never be.

But please pass on my congratulations to these splendid fellows and inform them that I will use this clever little sally in our next humorous discussion here at Eagle-Ho.

As ever,
DR. GOLF

34.

Dear Doctor Golf,

I am curious as to whether or not any notables in our generation come to Eagle-Ho. I am particularly interested in finding out about such men as Frank Sinatra, Dean Martin, Sammy Davis, Jr., Peter Lawford, Allen Freed, Steve Reeves.

JOSEPH HELLER
Brooklyn, N. Y.

Dear Sir,

If these men are notables their names have escaped me in the quarterlies and chronicles that I read. I assume these men are leaders of business and scholars. Unfortunately, we do not make a practice of divulging any names at Eagle-Ho.

DR. GOLF

35.

Dear Dr. Golf,

Once again we would like to call your attention to the fact that April 15 is the deadline for your Federal income tax payment. Since you have not favored us with a return since the Federal income tax law was passed in 1913, we feel certain that the outstanding balance must be considerable. We are also sure you understand how difficult it is for our accountant to keep these empty files open for so many years. Frankly, we feel that it is imperative at this time that you state precisely what you intend doing.

JAMES ELLIOTT
Department of the Treasury
Internal Revenue Service

Dear Sirs,

I intend doing precisely what I have been doing since your income tax law was passed in 1913 . . . nothing.

As ever,
DR. GOLF

36.

Dear Doctor Golf,

We were wondering who is your favorite writer and what is your favorite poem?

JOHN BERILE
Tulsa, Okla.

Dear Sir,

As to my favorite writer, I would instantly choose England and India's Rudyard Kipling. I find his "Gunga Din" and his "Road to Mandalay" manly, spirited and constantly invigorating. Occasionally we will have little programs here at Eagle-Ho in the evenings and I often favor my members with a rousing recitation of "Gunga Din." On special occasions I don the purple and gold of Eagle-Ho and sing "The Road to Mandalay." (Incidentally, the Eagle-Ho marching song is based on the music of "The Road to Mandalay.")

At Eagle-Ho, Rudyard Kipling is required reading and those few men who cannot enjoy him I usually find harboring some inherent weakness of fibre or soul that eventually results in their expulsion.

As ever,
DR. GOLF

37.

Dear Doctor Golf,

We have a very interesting selection of art studies and still photographs that the boys at Eagle-Ho might find extremely interesting. Also in short supply, but available at this time, is the premium film with sound of Hedy Lamarr in "Ecstasy."

Our usual stock of 16-mm. Mickey Mousers is listed in our catalog which I am enclosing.

JOHN P. COX
100 West 42nd St.
New York, N. Y.

Dear Sir,

Usually I do not answer any letters of solicitation, but yours, oddly enough, comes at a time when I do need some new films here at Eagle-Ho.

My members have seen all the Mickey Mouse cartoons and as far as I can determine all the others that are available in 16 mm. We are interested, however, in a number of "Our Gang" movies. If you could lay your hands on those I would be glad to pay any amount you think fair. We are also interested in the 15-part serial, "The Green Hornet."

As ever,
Dr. Golf

38.

Dear Doctor Golf,

While I am 44 years old, I have been playing golf for only 22 years. I do not play every day, but manage to get in from seven to nine complete rounds each week. My handicap is 14. It was 14 ten years ago and, as I look forward to the years ahead, I believe it will remain at 14 until I hole out for the last time.

Is it possible that I am wrong? Is there any chance for me to get a handicap drop as I get older? Please answer this question and also what in your opinion is the age when a man reaches his zenith in golf.

I enclose a few score cards and comments.

I remain,
Ebersole Gaines
Lake Forest, Ill.

Dear Sir,

The age when a man reaches his golf handicap climacteric cannot be pinned down so easily. Too many variables enter in. Obviously if you had not frittered away the patrimony of your youth and had started playing golf, say, at 7 instead of 22, you would have an additional 15 years to your advantage and in all likelihood you would have experienced another handicap drop some years ago.

Like the Greeks, I follow the numeral 7 and its multiplication to odd numbers to establish the cardinal years in a man's life and that time when he can expect dramatic changes. As example, 7 times 3 is 21; 7 times 4 is 28, etc., etc. The years we can then watch and expect significant transformations in are 21, 35, 49, 63, 77, 91, 105, 119 and 139.

And so in your case I believe in between 4 and 5 years, which will bring you to your 49th year, and a mere youngster in the game of golf, you will experience another handicap breakthrough. I have studied the score cards you submitted along with your analysis of each game and, based on those findings, I am positive that your 49th year will also bring a new number to your handicap block—11 or 9, possibly 8.

As ever,
DR. GOLF

39.

Dear Doctor Golf,

I am in my 65th year and I have been seized by golf like a mouse in the claws of a golden eagle. At first I fought it off, but now I am helpless in its grasp.

Doctor, I have never been a very strong or strong-willed man. In marriage I married the first pale shade that said yes. In business my natural timidity kept me on the lower rungs of the ladder. I suffer from dropsy, vertigo, chronic fatigue, and a total lack of ambition.

But all this is behind me, for now I golf. Golf has brought on a complete metamorphosis and I am delirious with joy. Now I rise at six, take a cold shower, eat a big breakfast and repair to the first tee. Every day, rain or shine, I get in 18 holes before noon. At noon I have an enormous lunch on the apron of the 18th green, take five minutes for the necessary ablutions and begin the next 18 and sometimes 27 holes before 12:30. I play alone. I need no company.

In short, despite my age and my handicap, which is 26, I am a complete golfer. You will refer to the first sentence in this letter. My question concerns age. Doctor, how much time have I left? I feel if I know I can better plan my rounds. If it's less than the ten or fifteen years I am counting on, I plan on playing 27 holes in the morning and trying for 36 in the afternoon. As I said, I play alone and keep the ball down the middle. I have clocked myself on a fast day and I can get in 18 holes in two hours flat.

I remain,
Charles Einstein
Oakland, Calif.

Dear Sir,

My hat is off to you. You are truly a man who has found himself. One of the maxims I uttered long ago, and one that has been accepted—if bastardized—by the golfing world at large, is that "golf is not, nor can it ever be, a young man's game." For it is as true now as it was then that it can never take less than 35 years to properly groove a swing. These years are necessary for many reasons and perhaps the one that

is the most important, and the one you are experiencing so poignantly, is the proper humility. This humility cannot come, nor can golf come, to the youthful.

It cannot come when that yeasty, raw turbulence is present. Indeed, it will not come until this yoke, this enemy, is cast out. For golf waits shyly outside the door while this being is present and it has to be coaxed inside with promises and sweetmeats.

Only after the fetters of youth have been flung aside can golf enter. Only then can the man know the folly of his adolescent belief of the swing answering to the man and perceive the joy and the truth of the complete man answering to the swing.

And, as the years and the eagles cascade by, the even greater joy is realized when he stands in the bright sunlight of complete fulfillment and comes to realize that the *swing is the man.*

Sir, there are no words, or metaphors, to express the ecstasy I daily experience when I gaze out and watch my lads in their 77th, their 91st, their 105th years plunging down the first fairway or sauntering up to the 18th green and cocking their score cards to get the last bit of sunlight. Why, sir, a man in his 65th year is a mere stripling here. If you were three years younger you would be called upon to do caddy duty. So, despair not about age.

Everything changes, fades and passes away. But one thing here is as constant as the globe, and that is the classic swing. Daily I see its wonderment in our members above 75. For by then the Eagle-Ho swing has been properly grooved for 35, 55, even 70 years, and now it is locked in place. The muscle, the bone, the brain, the very gene know nothing else. And these men, these stalwart, loyal followers who are in their golden age, have listened, have practiced, have learned; and now it can be said that if any man ever knew the game, these men truly do.

As ever,
Dr. Golf

40.

Dear Doctor Golf,

Is it true that the first American golf was played at 72 Street at Broadway in New York City in 1886 and two years later at St. Andrew's in Yonkers, N. Y.?

Robert E. Lee
Silvermine, Conn.

Dear Sir,

Your information is only partially correct. While John Reid, John Upham, Harry Holbrook, Kingman Putnam, and Henry Talmadge played in the field you describe in 1886, and St. Andrew's at Yonkers did come into being in 1888, golf at that time had been flourishing in Charleston, S. C., and Savannah, Georgia, for well over a hundred years.

The so-called golf authorities of today will shout that there are no records before the above date at St. Andrew's, but, if you are interested in facts rather than dismal records, please be advised that my great-grandfather visited this country in 1836 and had an 84 at the Charleston club. He also played the Savannah club, but he putted badly and kept no score. Down through the years the families that founded these two courses have supplied many members to Eagle-Ho and to Eagle-Ho International. Both of these clubs are, of course, Eagle-Ho approved. As a matter of incidental, but historic, fact, the Charleston and Savannah Railroad was expressly built to join these two fine clubs and to provide transportation between the tournaments and the festivals that were then flourishing.

The men who founded these clubs were not interested, nor are their families now interested, in who was first in this country—themselves or St. Andrew's. I am sure they would say, if they chose to say anything, that if St. Andrew's insists that they were first, well, let them then be first.

As ever,
Dr. Golf

P.S. I imagine that field at 72nd Street and Broadway would make a nice course. Are there any courses near that area or is it all now milk farms?

41.

Dear Doctor Golf,

In my parish here in Sussex we have a rather unique problem. The golfing members of my church have banded together and are practicing their own form of religion. Three months ago they erected a shrine to Eagle-Ho.

While I have never been allowed to attend their services I can imagine what goes on and I shudder to think of what form of ceremony is being used. A more visible sign of this defection is the wearing of your Eagle-Ho medallion around their necks.

At first I thought we were having a religious revival but, when I heard one of them incanting his strange golf prayer as he rubbed his medal, I knew we were in grave danger.

Already there is talk about the canonization of Mungo Park, Walter Travis, and your father, and a petition has been circulated entitled "The Handicap Miracle." I have spoken to the golf professional at the club and he states that there has been a severe rash of handicap lowerings during the past two fortnights.

It is my thinking that this has spurred on this flagrant and malignant heresy. I have had no communication from the east at this writing, but I expect one at any time. I beg of you, sir, speak out against this growing schism. They will listen only to you.

THE REV. THOMAS C. BEACH
Heathcotewoodshire, Sussex, England

Dear Sir,

I have checked with the club you are concerned about. This is an Eagle-Ho Approved establishment as are the members. The handicap drop came after the erection of the shrine. I can see no immediate problem in their concentrating on my medallion. This is a practice I teach and encourage, and one I find extremely helpful in freeing one's mind for the serious business of a difficult approach, a run-up shot or a long breaking putt. Perhaps I could suggest the same to you. It might take your mind off what you now feel is a growing problem.

In the unlikely event an Eagle-Ho cult does spring up, as did happen in Rhodesia in 1923, please feel free to notify me straightaway. But for the next ninety days I must insist that you do not interfere, regardless of how strange the practices appear to be. A denunciation at this time, from any quarter, could and possibly would have a more than serious effect on said members' handicaps.

As ever,
DR. GOLF

42.

Dear Doctor Golf,

We play golf here all winter. We use electric socks with pocket batteries and oil-filled hand warmers. Despite this, we are still cold and we tend to drink too much, which in turn ruins our games. Do you have any advice on keeping warm in the face of the freezing winds we encounter here.

> CARL WATSON
> Great Bluff, S. Dakota

Dear Sir,

While electric socks, etc., can answer the warming needs of one's extremities it is often at the expense of the main portions of the body remaining cold. Shoulders, chest, and lumbar cold is usually agonizing and it is always cumulative. I need not tell you of the deleterious effect this has on one's long iron game.

I have always recommended to my friends in the northern latitudes the use and portage of a stout charcoal brazier. This vessel should not be less than two feet in diameter nor should it hold less than sixty pounds of burning coke. This instrument, while it may appear primitive, is of an inestimable excellence to those who have suffered the pangs, the chilblains, and the rising handicap of winter golf.

There are two methods of carrying this brazier around the course. An extra brace of stout caddies equipped with asbestos-lined gloves is the most satisfactory. Failing this, two long wooden poles and a chain suspension will work. This second suggestion is to be used when the weights of the caddies fall below 75 pounds. In either event you are in for a most satisfying surprise. A resourceful caddy will

equip himself with provisions for manufacturing hot toddies, a simple roast, or a barbecue—or possibly chestnuts.

One precaution would be to send your fore caddy ahead and leave supplies of coke at the sixth and twelfth tees. As a rule of thumb, figure ten pounds of coke per hole when the wind is less than twenty knots per hour. Above twenty knots add one pound for every knot.

As ever,
DR. GOLF

43.

Dear Doctor Golf,

Two years ago you answered my problem of not keeping my right foot on the ground by sending me a 14-pound right shoe. The shoe has worked quite well, but now I am tired of wearing this ridiculous thing. I drag around the course like Quasimodo of Notre Dame, and since the shoe scars the greens I have to take it off before putting and then put it back on.

By the time I have completed 18 holes (and our course is very hilly), I have taken the shoe off 18 times, put it on 18 times, plus 2000 yards of detouring around streams and sands and irregular terrain, and I am too weary to post my score.

Added to this my problem has worsened. I have been experimenting at home without the shoe, and where I used to barely lift my foot at impact, it now flies upward. It now appears that I can never play without this device or one similar to it.

I have gotten used to, and can ignore, the many nicknames I enjoy at the club, viz., "Rumpelstiltskin," "The Man in the Iron Shoe," "Slue-Foot," etc.

Dr. Golf, I don't believe I can bring myself to give up playing golf, but I am finding it increasingly difficult to appear at the first tee with this insane device dragging behind me. If I have to go through another two years like the past two I am afraid my resources will be exhausted. I beg of you, is there not some other instrument, perhaps smaller, possibly of an internal nature, that I could use?

I remain,
RALPH LINVILLE
Monterey, Calif.

Dear Sir,

The directions for using Doctor Golf's Eagle-Ho leaded shoe (14 pounds) clearly state that you can remove weights gradually as the weeks go by. In three months after your first round you should have been down to your normal shoe weight. WHY you failed to follow these simple instructions is beyond me, for they are clearly stamped on the carton. I am enclosing an empty carton at no charge. Please follow the directions this time.

During the past two years I have perfected another instrument for keeping one's right or left foot in place during the swing. It consists of a simple steel eyehole made into the sole of the desired shoe. A series of steel rods, suitable for storing in golf bag, and a hammer complete the set. One has merely to line up one's shot and then have the caddy quickly drive the steel rod through the eyehole and into the ground. The length of the rods becomes shorter as one progresses and eventually one is back at the normal Eagle-Ho golf shoe.

Please keep me posted on your progress.

As ever,
DR. GOLF

44.

Dear Doctor Golf,

Our last hole here at Ardsley finishes with a spectacular view of the Hudson River. Two weeks ago a member, whose name I shall withhold, passed on. In the dead of night his family had him buried, as his will insisted, on the apron of the 18th green. His will also called for a bronze plaque to be placed at the grave. In the same will he donated a rather large amount of money to the club under the provisions that each detail of his burial be rigidly adhered to. You will be flattered to know that you were named arbiter in case of any subsequent problem. The problem must be handled carefully for the member's family are all nongolfers and know nothing of the difficulty of run-up shots.

In short, they have placed a one-foot by two-foot plaque flat on the apron directly in front of the center of the green. Our members cannot play pitch shots here, for beyond the green, as described earlier, is the Hudson.

We need the money our departed member left us, for now we are able to buy several holes that were previously leased. We would appreciate your advice on this delicate matter.

> We remain,
> GREENS COMMITTEE
> Ardsley Country Club
> Ardsley-on-Hudson, N. Y.

Dear Sirs,

This same member also left a rather sizable trust fund for me to administer in the raising and care of Eagle-Ho caddies, so I am fully aware of the man and his family. It is unfortunate that the family consists of nongolfers, but I am certain we can work out some equitable and workable solution.

My first reaction to your letter was one of concern, not for the problem of run-up shots, but for the 18th green itself. I am familiar with this course and I know this green well. I had discussed this entire matter with our departed friend several months ago. It was my understanding he would take up the proposition with the Greens Committee and it was my suggestion that he request a site far to the left of the

green and closer to the high ridge. As a matter of fact,
prior to our game he had considered turning the bulk
of his estate into a hospital fund, and a portion into a
stained glass window at one of the larger cathedrals
in New York City. I knew Ardsley's financial position
and took the liberty of insisting that he make over
his estate into a golf fund.

And so, when I heard the grave was directly in
front of the green in that low portion of the apron,
I was fearful that the drainage of the green might be

endangered. A subsequent examination of our friend's will assured me that all precautions had been taken.

I have drafted a letter to this man's family. I have also cited several pages from my pamphlet on "Golf Philanthropy." One of the most successful plans I have followed in the past is to recommend that the flag itself be imprinted with the donor's name. In other words, under the legend "18" there is sewn "in Memory of J. Smith" etc. A gold band can also be placed around the flagpole and the hole can be called "Smith's Hole" on the score card. Any or all of these can be done in the best of taste. I feel confident our deceased friend's family will not insist on the bronze plaque remaining where it is. In any event I am planning on being in the East in the next two months and shall make a point of inspecting the grave and calling on the family.

As ever,
DR. GOLF

45.

Dear Doctor Golf:

As a student of physical anthropology I was wondering if there is a golf type. What I mean to say is, are there some specific physical traits that are usually found in good golfers? In other words, if all things are equal among a variety of anthropological types, which would you pick as the golf type? I would sincerely appreciate any comments and would be grateful for any and all bibliographical references.

I remain,
RICHARD KERR
Mobile, Ala.

Dear Sir,

You won't be a student long; soon you will be a master, for you have already mastered the anthropological method of throwing a veil over a simple fact and extracting a thousand words where ten would suffice.

Yes, there is a golf type. Just as tall, dark men make good surgeons and pianists, and short, fat small-headed men become leaders of industries, there is a definite golf type. You will find him standing alone at parties. He is taller, his outward appearance can be called sadder, his hands hang quietly, and often he is gazing at a window or an object in the distance. There is a seriousness around the eyes and an honest brooding strength about the set of his jaw. I call this look the look of eagles. His mind is not on the petty, the commonplace, the Dow-Jones averages; he does not converse easily with women. If he drinks, it is the straight whiskeys—the bourbons, the Scotches, the Irish; never mixed drinks—the cocktail, the Manhattan or the Martini. He holds his head a little higher than the average. His cephalic index is 86.

There will be an absence of flesh, a high threshold of nervousness, and little inclination to entertain in the low manner of jokes, tricks with glasses, spoons, etc. He does not dance and seldom cares for any type of so-called modern music. He is, in short, a leader and since there is now so little to lead he remains on the periphery of the crowd. Economics and family require that he conform to a degree, but he keeps this to a minimum. And in his inner self, where he excludes all save golf and his golfing friends, he is gazing at the lovely green, the flowing fairway and the arching ball.

As ever,
DR. GOLF

46.

Dear Doctor Golf:

Is it my imagination or is it a fact that if you place two golfers (unknown to each other) in a room with forty other people they will eventually find each other. I have seen this happen over and over again and I have yet to discover what the secret is.

I remain,
Wm. Patterson
Dayton, Ohio

Dear Sir,

Enclosed is my letter of April to an anthropological journeyman regarding golf types. A few of the reasons why golfers attract golfers are here. There are more clues, but basically we are dealing with intangibles.

How can I describe the Look of Eagles, the aura of golf?

The cast in the eye, the thrust of the jaw, the relaxed shoulders and triceps—these are part of it, but there is more, much more. Often the feet will be squared, the weight balanced, and the knees slightly tucked, but these are surface things and of no consequence. There is something indescribable that pervades the whole being—a thing in itself, to borrow from Kant, that transcends and reveals him to golfers and to no one else.

I often liken it to the Biblical phrase concerning the astonished heart. But I can do little more than that. While I can compare it or list the outward manifestations, I, sir, cannot say what it is other than the outward appearance of an inner peace and joy.

As ever,
Dr. Golf

47.

Dear Doctor Golf:

I am 6′ 2″ tall, weight 190, and am 24 years old. I am delighted with my swing and often pose for golf clothing advertisements. All of the members here at Wykagyl Country Club say I have the most beautiful swing in Westchester County. I generate tremendous club head speed, have fantastic hands, and finish every shot high and well behind my neck. I do not wish to disturb my swing, but I would like to get more distance. Normally, I get from 75 to 85 yards off of the tee.

> GRENVILLE KEOGH
> Wykagyl Country Club

Dear Sir,

You are the victim of the standard hoax that often befalls men so consumed with vanity.

You are obviously using tennis balls.

> As ever,
> DR. GOLF

48.

Dear Doctor Golf:

Every year we here at the Foundation choose several men or institutions connected with the arts and sciences for a gift of either money or automobiles to be used as they see fit in carrying out their work. We have decided to grant you and Eagle-Ho a fleet (12) of Stutz station wagons. You may expect delivery during the next month. There are no conditions connected with this gift other than that we expect you and your followers to drive only Stutzes.

> FRANKLIN D. NOGURSKI
> The Bearcat Foundation

Dear Sir,

I appreciate your most generous offer, but I am afraid I must decline. Several years ago we were given a number of Rausch & Lang Electric Runabouts that have performed splendidly. The obvious reason, I'm sure you can see, is the lack of the internal combustion engine and the absence of any noise.

Thanking you for the offer, I remain

DR. GOLF

49.

Dear Doctor Golf,

During the past few months we have had an outbreak of moles here at our course. They rip up the fairways and tees and often erupt under a green causing considerable damage. Our greenskeeper is frantic. Can you give us any advice on this?

Sincerely,
JAMES DINAN
Newport, R. I.

Dear Sir,

Indeed I can. Contrary to popular thought, the star-nosed mole (*Condylura cristata*) which is prevalent in your section of the country and mine is in reality the greenskeeper's friend. A common fallacy is that they will kill off the earthworm which is believed to be beneficial due to its earth-turning qualities. While it is true that moles subsist on earthworms, it is also true that the avenues they choose to explore are that dry and brittle portion of the earth that earthworms cannot penetrate.

Often I will capture a mole or two and place him in a dry section of the fairway where neither earthworms nor water can penetrate. Within two weeks, the earth is soft and the grass verdant. If a geological cutaway of a properly laid green is studied, one immediately observes definite mole corridors down as low as fifteen feet. It is here the star-nosed mole does his greatest service to the green for no other animal, microbe, or instrument can effect this. They prefer to live in this deeper environment and, as you know, proper aeration begins in these areas. Since he prefers this depth, the mole seldom appears near the surface of the earth.

Only a mole who has lost his way or one who is deranged will enter directly under a green and cause damage. I am confident yours will not venture across your greens again.

As for the fairways and tees, please be assured that the mole knows what he is doing and if he chooses to disrupt a certain passage of grass it is for a very good reason. I would also suggest that you check with your greenskeeper; perhaps this fellow is not telling you all you should know. In the event the keeper has been slothful or slovenly, he may well be blaming our friend, the star-nosed mole, for his own shortcomings.

In the unlikely event of a deranged mole doing further damage, I would recommend a mole patrol to check the area at dusk. They should be equipped with stethoscopes, a brass triangle, and a steel rod. If the deranged mole is heard (the sound is an unmistakable grating, gargling noise), the men have only to strike the triangle with the rod. Moles cannot stand this sound and immediately take cover by plunging back down to their natural environment.

As ever,
Dr. Golf

50.

Dear Doctor Golf,

An Eagle-Ho member of yours told me that you have a practicing device which uses lighted firecrackers.

Could this be true? If so, please tell me about it.

Very Truly Yours,
JOHN KEMP
Lititz, Penna.

Dear Sir,

Unlike my many apparatuses for golf improvements here at Eagle-Ho, this device is not secret or patented. In short, anyone can do it with my compliments.

It is a very simple method for making a golfer concentrate. Assume the shot is a tee shot with a driver. One merely tapes three firecrackers with slightly different length fuses onto the top of the club head. The ball is then teed and the fuses lighted. It is ideal to have the first firecracker explode during address, second at top of back swing, and third at impact or during first part of follow-through. Since it is almost impossible to set the fuses to produce this effect, you will quickly see that the golfer will have no idea when the explosions will occur.

This confuses the golfer, who doesn't know when to expect these noises, and he soon learns to concentrate on hitting the ball. After a thorough training in this manner a man of firm character and fibre will develop an unshakable concentration that neither wind nor lightning can shatter.

As ever,
DR. GOLF

51.

Dear Doctor Golf,

Is there some trick in judging the distance between the ball and the flag? Often I can guess to within 15 yards. My friends all have the same problem. We were also wondering about the distance-judging feats of Walter Travis. Every account of his estimating yardage usually mentions that he had the power to determine within a yard on most distances. Was this some trick he learned or is there some procedure he followed to let him know this valuable information? If it was either of these, who taught him?

F. F. WOOD
Manhasset, N. Y.

Dear Sir,

Someone did tell Walter Travis how far the ball was from the flag and he told him often. Someone was there on every shot and whispered in his ear when he posed this question. That someone, sir, was the good Lord.

For Walter Travis was given this remarkable gift at birth. It came with the gene. It is a rare gift and it blooms like the century plant. It came in the early works of Sophocles, in the perfect circle of Giotto, to Scarlatti, Vivaldi, Bach, Shakespeare, Rudyard Kipling, and to my friend Walter Travis.

I teach a procedure that guarantees results within five yards, but I would never presume to enter the area of Travis. I know my limitations.

The method I teach, and it is long and complex, involves pressure, altitude, humidity, wind, shadows, and several optical integrations. I discourage this procedure, for usually the luggage and the operation of a psychrometer, an altimeter, a windometer, a slide rule, and miniature transit before each shot to a green saps the golfer's strength and dissipates his concentration to such a degree that his shots tend to slice or fade badly.

As an alternative, I would recommend a clipboard and a good supply of sharp pencils. Before each shot, estimate the distance and mark it down. Then, after the shot, measure the distance and mark that down. Following the day's round, plot the estimated yardage versus the actual yardage on a simple bar graph. In all likelihood you will find your estimates shorter than the actual. On your next day's round, increase your estimates by this degree, and so on.

As ever,
DR. GOLF

52.

Dear Doctor Golf,

In your letter last week on estimating yardage, you forgot to explain how one measures the actual yardage. I find your procedure excellent and I am already getting better results. Unfortunately, when I load my bag down with 250 yards of steel tape I have little room for my clubs. As a loyal Eagle-Ho member, I use only stout, submissive caddies so I have no trouble with the portage. But I feel there must be a better measuring device than steel tape. I tried cloth one day, but I need the rigidity of steel in the high winds we have lately been having.

F. F. WOOD

Dear Sir,

I found it difficult to believe that an Eagle-Ho member did not know how to measure yardage and ran an immediate check on your scholastic record. I was shocked to find that in the years you were taking instructions at the Long Island Eagle-Ho chapter this course was not taught. I have taken this matter up with my board and directives will soon be going out. In the meantime, all Long Island Eagle-Ho members will be required to stand by on a probationary basis until this requirement is passed.

I would advise that you begin practicing in earnest at once. Failure to pass this test will, of course, result in revocation of cards and privileges and loss of seniority. A practice you might try at home to acquaint yourself with this is as follows:

Get a stencil impression made of your left and right shoes and sufficient paint or dye to contrast with your floors, walks, rugs, etc. Lay out the left and right shoe patterns in your house and yard and anywhere you do much walking. Measure carefully between each stencil so the distance is exactly 36″ from the heel of your right foot to the toe of your left.

You are now ready to practice the Eagle-Ho 36″ stride. Practice at least 40 hours (it may be a difficult adjustment if you are immoderately tall or short) before venturing out on an unmarked area. A simple back and forth pattern between the living room and the kitchen will be satisfactory in the evenings, but in the day you must get the feel of the 36″ stride in the open air.

Carry 30 or 40 feet of steel tape (no more than this) to your office. Measure there, stencil there, and if it is necessary to close and lock your door, do so, but you must make the time and space available so you can stride there. When you come upon an unknown area, pause before crossing and estimate the yardage. After you cross, stop and measure back to the beginning. You will find many ways, as you go along, to practice and check on yourself.

Often it's best to work in pairs. Contact another Eagle-Ho member in Long Island (there are 97 at large on the same membership probation as you). Check one another and then go on to a third and a fourth member. Try walking in groups. If someone plays a musical instrument, say a mouth organ, have him lead you in a marching-type song and sing lustily as you practice the stride.

In the event your height is about 6′ 1″, I would advise strapping and containing the knees with a homemade leather belt device. Once again I call your attention to Article 412, paragraph two, in the Eagle-Ho Handbook: "The official Eagle-Ho stride is 36″ in the United States of America. In England, it will remain at 39.37″ until such time as the metric system is abolished."

As ever,
DR. GOLF

53.

Dear Doctor Golf,

Several unanswered questions keep coming up during our meetings of the Ways and Means Committee. These questions concern your relations and activities with the President. I am sure you can see the gravity and the seriousness of this situation and I trust that you will be helpful and at the same time treat the matter as highly confidential. For your convenience I will list the questions:

1. Whose idea was it that the protocol commit-

tee recognize you as an honorary Cabinet member?

2. Was the Presidential plane ever named "Eagle-Ho"?

3. Did you supervise the laying of the green on the White House lawn?

4. Is there a Presidential suite of rooms at Eagle-Ho?

5. Were you instrumental in the lobby that pushed the bill through that the President could not serve three terms? In particular, did you or did you not tell this same lobby that a third term would bring about a definite rise in handicap?

6. Was there at any time a "hot wire" from Washington and Augusta to Eagle-Ho?

7. Since January 15th, how many months has the President been at Eagle-Ho?

ALBERT DONOVAN
Washington, D. C.

Dear Sir,

For your convenience, I will make my answer very short: No comment.

As ever,
DR. GOLF

54.

Dear Doctor Golf,

Throughout your letters I denote a disapproval of public courses. As a golfer who has played both public and private courses I would like your candid opinion of public and private golf. . . .

NICHOLAS SMITH
Charleston, S. C.

Dear Mr. Smith,

Had you read all of my letters over the past years there would be no question as to the low opinion I have of public golf courses. If there is an opinion lower than the one I have of public courses it is the one I have of public golf. At my club we have 39 members. We have had 39 members here since the club was founded in 1898. Only when a member dies and a reasonable time has elapsed do we take in a new member. By keeping the membership to this number our fairways, tees and greens stay in excellent shape. There are no divot holes, pockmarked greens, and footprints in the sand traps; and if one feels like a shower and massage and possibly a nap between the 9th green and the 10th tee there is no problem of slowing the play. While some clubs, I am sure, cannot support the facilities of a large course with 39 members I have always advised that a membership never exceed 95. As a matter of fact I consider any club with an excess of 100 members to be a public course. My axiom as regards this is A PRIVATE COURSE OR NO GOLF.

Golf should be approached with humility, with respect; indeed, reverence. It should also be approached from a great distance with preparation, proper equipment, and proper clothing. Mass golf like any mass product is, by its very nature, banal. If a man cannot afford to have his clothes and clubs made to order by recognized, competent men he should never take up the game. Mass-produced woods and irons are the lowest form of this defection.

The very idea of clubs and balls in sports stores and drugstores sends chills down my spine. We have spawned a new Babylon with our driving ranges with their flamboyant-trousered, sunglassed, puce-faced professional who specializes in one club—the driver;

the miniature course, the lighted course, the putting
course—win a case of beer, win a clock radio—the
furred and frivolous wood covers, the plastic golf bag,
the zipper, the tasseled shoe, the obstreperous hats
and that most sordid, most foul, most lamentable of
all objects—the caddy cart!

If thru some strange, secret series of misunder-
standings a caddy cart were made to appear at some

point at my club there would be floggings and more floggings. And all these golfers. Golfers! Ha! I say. Hitters, punchers, lungers, stabbers; golfers none. With the exception of my students, whom I forbid playing in *any public* tournament, who do we have? No one. . . . Since Vardon and Jones, with the possible exception of that upstart Young Hagen, there have been no golfers in this country. I tell you that the time has come to plow up these fields, sow salt, and begin with the floggings.

As ever,
DR. GOLF

55.

Dear Doctor Golf:

By the time you receive this letter I will have amassed over 5000 hours on the practice tee with my professional, Mr. H. Levitt, here at the Glen Moor Country Club. I have been working on a dipping tendency that has plagued me for over four years. Five thousand hours times eight dollars per hour comes to 40,000 dollars, which you must admit is a considerable sum to spend on one flaw in a swing. I am not complaining about the money or the hours on the tee, I am complaining about the dip which is now more chronic than ever. Nothing prevents it and I have reached a point where I am afraid to venture out on the course and now spend all my golfing hours on the practice tee experimenting with stances, grips and various levels of swings. Incidentally, the pro has given me up and has passed my case to another professional (his son). Doctor, can you give me any advice?

WILLIAM GARDELLA
Little Grove, Ark.

Dear Mr. Gardella,

There is indeed nothing more serious or more difficult to correct than a violent dip. I take it by the tenor of your letter that yours is what I would term a violent dip. This is a strange phenomenon and an area of study certainly worthy of a thesis. Often the analysis and the cure take months. Unless I could see movies of your swing it would be hard for me to recommend a corrective device. Of course there is a good chance if your dip is of sufficient violence that we may be able to harness the expended energy and direct it into your swing.

Briefly, I would recommend using clubs substantially shorter, say eight to ten inches. This would allow for the dip and would harness the additional power you are generating with your lower abdomen. At first your swing might appear strange to the casual glance, possibly you might think it compared to a lunge more than a swing, but eventually when you see the longer drives you would be getting and the new crisp quality to the irons, I am sure you will be able to overlook this unusual appearance and enjoy your game as never before.

As ever,
Dr. Golf

P.S. Discharge this leechlike family of professionals immediately.

56.

Dear Dr. Golf:

Down here in Yoknapawtapha County there is a saying that as long as whiskey is made in the mountains all Swope golfers will have whistling back swings and boomerang hooks. I have a fast back swing, my father had one, and I've heard that my grandfather had one so fast it would pull his right foot off the ground. In the past year my son Coley Leroy, age 11 or 12, has come home and has taken up golf. Doctor Golf, young Coley Leroy whips it back so fast you can't even see it. I was wondering if a thing like this could have been inherited.

Joseph Swope
Irmo, Miss.

Dear Sir,

A fine putting touch, a sense of distance, a knowledge of proper irons—even an appreciation of the game of golf itself—have been scientifically proven to be inherited. The old golfing families have been aware of this for generations and have searched for these qualities in their offspring long before plans of marriage were discussed. Any competent genealogical study of the golfing families of Scotland will bear this out.

Unfortunately, just as good marriages produce low handicappers, poor marriages produce the duffers who crowd and devastate the land today. In golf the sins of our fathers cannot be concealed. I have only to gaze upon a slicer, a bobber, a swayer; and I can tell you from what foul stock the wretch sprang.

Mr. Swope, this is a very serious manifestation and it will need a serious method of correcting. I would suggest you visit your local genealogist and pursue this matter there. Possibly, you will not be able to do anything about your son. He may have to give up the game altogether. But out of this lesson may spring the seeds of greater Swope golfers in the generations to come. The sacrifice of your son's game may be a terrible price to pay, but I am afraid the damage has gone too deep. Often I will repair damage to the tissue, to the muscle; often the mental process through stimulation and therapy can be made to change and continue along a harmonious path, but when we begin tampering with the blood and the very gene itself we are in an area I chose not to enter.

Later, when your son contemplates matrimony I would advise you sending me along his fiancée's portfolio. I would be happy to advise you on this matter at no charge.

As ever,

Dr. Golf

57.

Dear Dr. Golf,

My name is Irving Mengel. I am 29 and I enjoy a handicap of 8 at the Split Rock course in New Jersey. Two years ago I discovered I was born under the astrological sign of Aries. I have been following the charts and predictions extremely close and I am having fantastic success with everything I plan in advance.

Do you have or is there available any horoscope literature having to do with golf?

I remain,
IRVING MENGEL
Hopewell, N. J.

Dear Sir,

There is and I am sending it to you at once. We publish here at Eagle-Ho a complete yearly volume and a monthly volume. I am sure you will find the monthly exceedingly helpful for it is broken down by sign, day of the month and golf handicap. I feel I can state without fear of successful contradiction that I am the only man in the world publishing this form of horoscope for golfers.

The response to this service in the past 16 years has been overwhelming and here at Eagle-Ho we have had to build a special wing to house the facilities for maintaining these periodicals.

You will receive the Doctor Golf Eagle-Ho yearly Astrological Chart $6.90 C.O.D. as well as the Doctor Golf Eagle-Ho Golfer's Monthly Horoscope $2.80. Incidentally, I, too, am an Aries.

As ever,
DR. GOLF

58.

Dear Doctor Golf,

I have been a member of the Greater Long Island Chapter of Eagle-Ho for nine years. I am now interested in Eagle-Ho Sanctuary. Since there is no advertising about this place, I was wondering if you would send me some literature, travel folders, and general information.

S. SILBAH
Great Neck, N. Y.

Dear Mr. Silbah,

What is Eagle-Ho Sanctuary? Sir, I find this question obscene. What is Versailles, what is Chartres, Mont-Saint-Michel? What indeed is the Benedictine Order?

There are answers, of course, but they entail volumes, art histories as well as the lives of famous men. Sir, there is no description of Eagle-Ho Sanctuary. If you would like to visit (one-day visits permissible to nine-year members in your classification) it might be arranged.

True, I could give you physical dimensions. I could say we have four great courses. But what is "great"? Are these courses great because every square foot of fairway and rough, every inch of tees and greens was brought over from Scotland in the early part of this century? Some people would choose not to believe that this makes a course great. And they would be right. If I told you eight hundred men worked nine years laying this sod, blending this moss, oats and Scottish heath; hand-watering, hand-dressing every tee, green, apron and fairway—this, too, might sound fanciful.

Since I allow no photography of any part of Eagle-Ho there is no way you can evaluate this except by a visit. We sleep two hundred and fifty guests. Each has a private room and terrace. Each has an attendant and a permanent caddy. Each has an individually tailored putting green. We have cobblers, ball makers, psychologists, a psychiatric testing clinic, hydrotherapeutic baths, shock treatment, etc.

But why go on? A list of such magnitude only confuses. For those who have visited, for those who have thrown off the troubles, the deceits, the noises, and the pursuit of the squalid meaningless values of the outside world and remained on here at Eagle-Ho for twenty, forty, indeed sixty years, I need no list, no brochure of advertising. I, sir, plan never to leave Eagle-Ho. Here I, as well as my many members, know peace, friendship, and the glorious feeling of fulfillment.

If you are interested in visiting us you will have to fill out the necessary applications, get three 15-year Doctor Golf sponsors and one Eagle-Ho Sanctuary permanent member, along with a detailed and full account of your concern and convincing evidence of why you would like to join us. We make the requirements exceedingly demanding because of the exceptional standard of excellence we maintain here at Eagle-Ho.

At this time we have no openings and our waiting list is now at five years. Needless to say our only membership vacancies are caused by the decease of a member.

I will be happy to take your application, etc., Mr. Silbah, but of course at this time I can promise nothing.

As ever,

Dr. Golf

59.

Dear Doctor Golf,

I have just played the Doctor Golf Eagle-Ho course at Eagle-Ho, Arkansas. There is a strong resemblance between this course and the King's Course near Edinburgh. I am wondering if Eagle-Ho is a copy of the King's Course?

DANIEL SANGSTER
Ames, Iowa

Dear Mr. Sangster,

There is a resemblance. There should be. Mr. S. McGregor copied Eagle-Ho in 1916. Every green, fairway, trap; every dogleg, water hazard—everything was photographed, drawn to scale and reconstructed north of Edinburgh on what is now called the King's Course. This, again, was one of those verbal agreements that never came to fruition. McGregor gave me his word that he would give me credit on the club plaque. It was to read "Course designed and recommended by Doctor Golf. A copy of Eagle-Ho, Eagle-Ho, Ark."

Mr. Sangster, the years go by too fast and I am far too busy with my students to contest this deceit. If Mr. McGregor has found it possible to live with his conscience these past years—well, sir, all I can say is he's not Eagle-Ho material. I have been perfectly willing to forget this matter, but in the past few months a new development has occurred. Unknown to anyone at the so-called King's Course, Mr. McGregor has sold off the first five holes to a real estate firm. In short, this course has a lifespan of maybe another six months.

One of the lesser tournaments, the British 4-Ball,

is played here every spring. St. Andrews has been alerted to this sale and has been in touch with me every day for the past month. Mr. Sangster, I plan to announce shortly that next year's British 4-Ball will be held at Eagle-Ho in Eagle-Ho, Arkansas. At that time the details of the theft, the deceit and the shallowness of Mr. S. McGregor will be made public.

Dr. Golf

60.

Dear Doctor Golf,

What is the true story about your match in 1932 with Holbrook and Darwin?

Robert O'Houlihan
New Orleans, La.

Dear Mr. O'Houlihan,

I have kept this match secret for over thirty years now protecting the honor of a then young Charleston girl it was my pleasure to have met at the Jeb Stuart Centennial in 1928. Now it can be told.

I played against Holbrook and Darwin's best ball on the Augusta National Course in the late spring of 1931. This was a private match and the only witnesses were the three young caddies present. My game, I must admit, was on and at the end of sixteen holes Holbrook and Darwin were eleven down. As we approached the eighteenth tee Holbrook informed me that he was in possession of some letters and photographs that, if placed in the wrong hands, could compromise the reputation of this certain young lady. Mind you, the lady was blameless, but Charleston society being what it was and with my knowledge of the nefarious Holbrook, I could see no alternative but to go along with Holbrook's scheme. Needless to say I agreed to falsify the score. I allowed them to win the eighteenth hole. As Darwin holed out his putt for a par 4 Holbrook loudly announced to the gallery that had formed around the green that he and Darwin had closed me out on the fourteenth green.

Since that day I have never spoken to Mr. Josiah Holbrook. His many apologies and requests for Eagle-Ho equipment are mailed back to him unopened. I accepted Mr. B. Darwin's apology and to this day we have remained great friends. I have buried the sordid memory of this infamous match for far too many years. Now that this lady is out of the way of mortal scandal I accuse Mr. Josiah Holbrook of one of the foulest breaches of golf in history.

I am having this accusation printed and posted in all of the important clubs in this country and England.

Dr. Golf

P.S. I have often wondered what Mr. Holbrook did with those three young caddies. . . .

61.

Dear Doctor Golf,

As a scholar of anthropology I was rather amazed and puzzled about the reports I have been hearing that you are employing Watusi Negroes from Dahomey, Africa, as caddies at your Eagle-Ho course in Eagle-Ho, Arkansas. I would be most grateful for any information you would like to pass on to me about these people. As you know I have written several extensive volumes on the history of the Watusi.

DR. H. FRONTIER
Harvard

Dear Dr. Frontier,

You are right, sir. We do employ Watusi Negroes as caddies at Eagle-Ho.

DR. GOLF

62.

Dear Doctor Golf,

I have been using Doctor Golf Eagle-Ho golf balls for seventeen years.

Last week, on an impulse, I cut one open to find out how they were so well made. I found it stuffed with feathers.

Would you please tell me how this is done.

PHIL CAMMARATA
Louisville, Ky.

Dear Mr. Cammarata,

Eagle-Ho balls are made in the same manner they were made in the eighteenth century in Scotland. True, we now make them faster. But basically they consist of young chicken, guinea, and plover feathers soaked in a brine solution with honey and beeswax. The combination of feathers, the degree of saline saturation, and the application of the honey and beeswax are, of course, confidential. We utilize no synthetics, and all of the work is of course done by hand.

As ever,
DR. GOLF

63.

Dear Doctor Golf,

How would you compare Wilson, Spaulding and Titleist balls to your own Eagle-Ho ball?

A. DONOVAN
Holyoke, Mass.

Dear Mr. Donovan,

Since I have never recognized either Wilson, Spaulding or Titleist as a legitimate manufacturer of golf balls or, for that matter, golf equipment, I would, sir, have no way of comparing.

I am told that these companies do exist and do make sporting equipment for baseball and football. However, until the time comes when they enter the golf field and my staff feels the quality of the balls or equipment sufficiently high enough to test against our products, I can only wait.

If, through some quirk of fate or some fantastic marketing blunder, they entered this field and chose to compete with Eagle-Ho I would be the last man in the world to discourage them until I had had a proper time to evaluate their efforts.

As ever,
DR. GOLF

64.

Dear Doctor Golf,

Do you recommend lifting weights to build up strength between seasons?

MR. KINGSLEY PEPPER
Flat Plains, Ga.

Dear Mr. Pepper,

First of all, there is no season in golf. Golf as I know and teach it knows no season. If my students can't afford to go south in the winter to play, I recommend giving up the game.

As for lifting weights at any time, I say, Bah! Lifting weights promotes homosexuality and very little else. If Eagle-Ho equipment is used, if Doctor Golf Eagle-Ho instructions are followed, if the workouts, the diets, the systems, machines and procedures are made available—there is no need for any additional strength.

My Eagle-Ho swing adapts itself to you and becomes so much a part of you that age, gout, fatigue, etc., have little or no effect on the swing. The swing by its very nature transcends the human form. The swing is there when you pass on. The idea of improving it with weight lifting or detracting from it by some other method is absurd. The swing, sir —my Eagle-Ho swing—is like the blue in the sky, immutable, eternal, indeed transcendental. Under no conditions, sir, would I ever recommend lifting weights.

As ever,
DR. GOLF

65.

Dear Doctor Golf,

As a child I always slept on my left arm. I guess this was because there was always a light on in the hall and I was afraid of the dark. Even to this day, while I am thirty-four years old, five feet eight and weigh 160 pounds in my stocking feet, I am still afraid of the dark. Occasionally my left arm would go to sleep and for long periods of time I had such pains, like hot and cold flashes and other things. I did real well in junior high school and the first two years in high school, but I didn't like the teachers in the eleventh and twelfth grades. Another interesting thing . . . I used to crack the knuckles on my left hand but never my right—wasn't that odd?

Perhaps this is the background for my problem, perhaps not. It's my left arm. That's where my problem is. You see it collapses on my back swing and

remains collapsed throughout the swing. Only after the ball is hit and dribbling toward the rough (I don't get much distance) and I am in the last part of my follow-through, do I get any feeling of stiffness and authority. I am sure this is not right.

Very truly yours,
Don Wine
Montauk, La.

Dear Mr. Wine,

What a fascinating letter. I, too, slept on my left arm as a child and for the very same reason. And, incredible as it may sound, I also cracked my left-hand knuckles. Were you by any chance born in April? If so, what day?

I am sending you my Doctor Golf Eagle-Ho left arm manacle, priced at $86.83. This is an ingenious apparatus of steel rods and leather braces for stiffening the left arm. I suggest wearing it around the house in increasing increments of time to get used to it.

You are cautioned also that this device, while stiffening the left arm, does by its very nature partially immobilize the left side of the body.

A handbook on how to plan your day, e.g., lighting a cigarette, using handkerchief, sudden moves, inadvisability of bending etc., is enclosed.

You are further cautioned to avoid driving and, if it is absolutely necessary to ride in an automobile, it will, of course, be necessary to sit in the rear seat.

Since this device is rather bulky, I am sending an oversized Doctor Golf Eagle-Ho jacket for wearing over it during actual play.

Don't forget to send me your birth date.

As ever,
Dr. Golf

66.

Dear Doctor Golf,

Do you have any general information about how to develop or maintain a proper golf deportment?
GEORGE STEVENS
Princeton

Dear Mr. Stevens,

How fortunate you are, Mr. Stevens, to be at Princeton. A marvelous school, a marvelous library. You, sir, will have little trouble in securing one of my guides and textbooks over the past forty years, Mr. John Cowan's "The Science of a New Life" published by J. S. Ogilvie.

For you who are less fortunate than Mr. Stevens, I quote the following which is as true now as it was in the last century:

"During my university career my passions were very strong, sometimes almost uncontrollable, but I have the satisfaction of thinking that I mastered them. It was however, by great efforts. I was the best oar of my year and when I felt particularly strong sexual desires, I sallied out to take more exercise. I was victorious always, and I never committed fornication. You see in what robust health I am. It was exercise that alone saved me.

"I may mention that I took a most excellent degree, and have reached the highest point of my profession. Here is an instance of what energy of character, indomitable perseverance, and good health will effect. To recapitulate in as few words as possible, the following are to be strictly avoided by those whose desire it is to lead a pure, chaste, and continent life: tobacco in all its forms, all manners of alcoholic liquors, late suppers and overeating, sweet-meats, candies, etc., white bread when it is possible to get the graham, pork, and all fat and salt meats, sausages, pickles, oysters, lobsters, eels, etc. Salt, except in moderate quantities, pepper, mustard, spices, vinegar, and other condiments; mince and other pies, and all manner of pastry; tea, coffee and chocolate; all constriction of dress about the body; idleness and inaction of body and mind; featherbeds and pillows, and heavy bed coverings, unventilated and unlighted bedrooms; remaining in bed in the morning after awaking; companions of doubtful or bad natures; irresolute will; uncleanliness of body, Turkish and Russian baths; drugs and patent medicines.

"In the foregoing list there are many things that the majority of mankind will think twice about before relinquishing their use. Yet to the individual whose desire is for a true life each and every item of the list must be discarded. There is not an article of food, condiment, or so-called luxury mentioned above that is in the remotest way necessary to the growth and nourishment of a healthy body and soul.

"I assert that any person disregarding, in whole or in part, the foregoing Plan of Life cannot be healthy, chaste, continent or even a Christian. A man cannot have a pure, clean, lovable soul in a foul, filthy body, and purity of soul is essentially requisite in a good Christian.

"Therefore, O man young and hopeful . . . O woman fair and trusting, see to it that you discard and avoid these abominations of modern civilization, and use, observe and enjoy only that required for your growth, purity and health of body and soul."

Here ends Mr. Cowan's lecture. There is nothing I can add to this.

As ever,
Dr. Golf

67.

Dear Doctor Golf,

I understand you conduct funerals at Eagle-Ho Sanctuary in almost a military manner. As a member of the Third Brigade of the Coldstream Guards I would be most happy to hear how this is done. Also, can one be buried at Eagle-Ho as a nonresident?

SIR HUBERT EARHART
K.C.B., Lt. Gen. (Ret.)
Cleveland, Ohio

Dear Gen. Earhart,

One cannot be buried at Eagle-Ho unless one has been a resident and a charter member for at least five years. True, we have many acres here at Eagle-Ho, but no resting place is considered satisfactory unless it meets with my unqualified approval. By virtue of this we confine all interments to those Eagle-Ho members who have qualified.

As for the military funeral, we have adopted the flanking and processional movements, with refinements of course, of the Black Hussars of Her Majesty's India Corps. Pallbearers are dressed in the official Eagle-Ho uniform, and the casket is carried on the shoulders in Hussar fashion.

Here the similarity ends. At Eagle-Ho most of our members prefer to be buried with their clubs and golf shoes. Each case may vary and often we fill the deceased golfer's trouser pockets with balls and tees.

Generally a crossed driver and spoon or midiron and putter are laid across the chest. After the casket is in position, three balls are teed up on either side and six Eagle-Ho golfers step forward.

It is, sir, a wonderful sight to see. The invocation, the Golfer's Creed and the Eagle-Ho pledge are read. The left drivers begin first from front to rear. Each steps forward slowly, adjusting his glove and studying the wind, takes his stance and cracks out a drive over the casket and into the distance.

A minute elapses between each shot until the last ball is driven. Following this, the men touch drivers across the grave in the same manner as foils are crossed at a military wedding and the golfer is lowered.

There is no mourning here at Eagle-Ho. We are far too busy. That very day an 18-hole best-ball tournament is held in honor of the absent golfer. Later, a bronze plaque is placed on his stone with a record of his fifty best scores, his three longest drives, and his list of eagles.

And then it is over.

As ever,
DR. GOLF

68.

Dear Doctor Golf,

How much help should one reasonably expect from a caddy on reading greens?
ROBERT CONWAY
Rye, N. Y.

Dear Mr. Conway,

A good caddy—one who has been properly broken in, trained and, of course, well groomed —should give incalculable assistance on the greens. His duties not only require that he be able to advise his master on direction and amount of break but also the firmness or softness of imparting the club to the ball.

To evaluate and advise, a caddy should be, and at Eagle-Ho we deem it mandatory, knowledgeable in the following:

1. Type and grain of grass. This does not mean merely identifying but a thorough understanding of the biology (perhaps etiology would be a better

word), of the nature of the green. He should be able to forecast effects of wind, rain, excessive dryness, results of particular types of pollenization, etc., etc.

2. A caddy should carry a psychrometer with him at all times and be skillful in its use to determine amount of moisture in the air directly above the green. Moisture will of course vary from shadowy areas to sunny areas and here the caddy should take several readings, compute the average, and arrive at a mode. There is a simple calculus formula for integrating this which it is advisable for all caddies to know. In many cases a ball's line will be through sun and shadow in varying amounts which obviously will slow and speed a ball in different increments. This rather tricky formulation is based on a rather complex ballistic integration. Once it is learned, however, the results are more than gratifying.

3. Two more lessons my International Caddy Corps utilizes with considerable success are detecting salinity in greens, and the simple but often overlooked physical law of gravitational pull. Salinity is too complex to discuss at this time and involves a rather complicated procedure. But a word on gravitational pull might be worthwhile here. A simple example of this would be the witnessing of water draining from a bath tub. In the northern hemisphere the water circles from left to right in the vortex. The converse of this is true in the southern hemisphere. Often this simple little axiom is overlooked and many have been the times that I've been aroused in the middle of the night by some frantic professional playing in Santiago or Johannesburg lamenting the sad state of his putting game. I need only remind him to reverse the line on all putts. The next day I usually find a lengthy cablegram of heartfelt thanks.

I had one particularly gifted lad at Eagle-Ho who when approaching a green would, without removing my bag from his shoulders, go down on his knees on the apron and smell the green. By virtue of this, this amazing chap could tell moisture, salinity, coarseness, effect of recent rain, wind, or fertilizer or excessive amounts of pollen. While this is an unusual case, I train *all* caddies at Eagle-Ho to become familiar with the taste of a green. A small portion properly chewed, with the background knowledge I have mentioned above, works wonders.

But all this is only an infinitesimal scratch on the surface of this most complex science. It is not enough for one to be able to merely "read" a green. One must in fact do more . . . one must "know" a green.

My books on reading greens are too numerous to list at this point. As a starter I would recommend the three volume "Reading Greens." This set is leather-bound and boxed with forty-six beautiful illustrations of this information in action. Complete set $14.30 C.O.D., postage $2.40.

As ever,
Dr. Golf

69.

Dear Doctor Golf,

Is Eagle-Ho Sanctuary on the Diner's Club Plan or American Express?

Very Truly Yours,
Happy Felton
West 44th St., N.Y.C.

Dear Mr. Felton,

I referred your question to my accountants and lawyers who are more worldly men than I. Unfortunately they, too, were unable to understand your question.

Perhaps you have misdirected this enquiry.

As ever,
Dr. Golf

70.

Dear Doctor Golf,

I am ninety-six years old and have shortened my swing until, alas, it is little more than waist high. Any day now I feel I will be standing on my last green with your Eagle-Ho putter in hand and holing out for the last time.

I have played many years and I have played well. Now that my friends have all gone I, too, am ready for my last nine. As a resident member at Eagle-Ho Sanctuary from 1921 to 1959 I am entitled to a resting place there. I would now like to know what to expect.

Sincerely,
Emory C. Emory
Short Hills, N. J.

Dear Mr. Emory,

My swing, my dear Emory, is neither as full nor as bold as it was that memorable day in 1926 when I had the great pleasure of witnessing that magnificent brassie shot that you holed out on Number 14 on the Glen Eagles Course for—a double eagle. That shot and our many games together are among my most treasured memories.

Emory, I visited your resting place last month and on gazing at it I must admit to a deep feeling of satisfaction and pride. First of all, it overlooks Glen Eagles and offers a view of the 14th fairway and green, the scene of your unforgettable shot. Of course you know there are chestnut trees and golden maple, cypress, and our own exquisite variety of loblolly pine.

Your place is on a high hill and when the leaves fall in November you can count the seventy-two flags on the four great courses that gave you so much pleasure.

In the spring, when the peach and apple trees have bloomed and their colors are as loud as lions and as soft as fog and you hear the sounds of the drives, the midirons' unmistakable crack, and the full-throated "Fore" echoing and re-echoing through the woods and perfect glens . . . then Emory you will know you are truly home.

As ever,
Dr. Golf

71.

Dear Doctor Golf,

In your letter of August 4, 1960 to one Amos Jones of New York City you stated and I quote:

"In the hallway at Eagle-Ho, across from the bust of Vardon and beneath the death masks of the great Scots, lies the putter of Walter Travis."

This cannot be, for this summer while traveling in Sandwich I visited the Royal St. George Course and there I saw Travis's putter in their Hall of Fame. I am enclosing a picture of same.

Doctor Golf, I have long been an admirer of

yours and I have never had occasion to question your authority or scholarship, but in this instance I must insist you print an immediate apology for this gross and misleading statement.

I remain,
DAVID EVANS
Bar Harbor, Maine

Dear Sir,

In my house there are many putters. All of which are properly catalogued according to player, tournament and year. I have had the photograph you mailed blown up and have studied the putter at some length. If ever I erred in using Walter Travis's name, believe me, sir, my apologies and lamentations would be long and loud.

You are, however, correct about a putter of his lying in state at Royal St. George, but you are only partially correct. The putter you were privileged to see and photograph at Royal St. George was the putter Walter called "The Schenectady." Upon close examination and checking my files I find that this is the club he used at Brookline when he defeated Ted Ray and Vardon. At this particular match Travis was in a putting slump and had contacted me. I met him at Brookline and immediately suggested his using this center-shafted club. He followed this advice and I, in turn, followed him around the last eighteen holes advising him on position and pointing out the rather tricky breaks in the green. At one point, Vardon asked the judges to disqualify Travis because of my presence, but this was turned down.

Following this victory Travis gave me the putter for Eagle-Ho. Later at dinner Walter and I were approached by Maxwell O'Hallahan of Royal St. George. He offered me eighteen greens delivered to

Eagle-Ho for the putter. Travis, knowing the quality of the Scottish green and the expense of shipping eighteen of them halfway around the world, insisted that I accept the offer. The eighteen greens were placed in 1921 on our now famous Glen Eagles Course.

Glen Eagles later became Travis's favorite course and many were the times he and I, and occasionally Ray, played it. To this day Travis's magnificent 69, from the back tees with the course measuring well over 7400 yards, stands as a course record.

And so, dear sir, while Royal St. George has one putter of Travis's I have seventeen, along with a number of pairs of shoes, a bronze relief of his grip, several hundred photographs and score cards, and memories, sir, that are beyond the glass cage, and the bronzes and yellowing daguerreotypes.

As ever,
Dr. Golf

72.

Dear Doctor Golf,

Our club here at Ardsley has been Eagle-Ho approved since 1927. All clubs are wooden shafted, all equipment is Eagle-Ho; our caddies are properly liveried and obedient, caddy flogging flourishes, and we have not tolerated carrying doubles or the professional fraternizing with the members. You would think that with all these fine recommendations and our maintaining the required ninety-two members we would have no problems.

Such is not the case. Four of our most ambitious, most generous and loyal members have made the course virtually unplayable. They tee off at 9 A.M.

and hole out on the eighteenth long after six o'clock. We on the Greens Committee are in perfect accord with the fact that some foursomes play slower than others, and that a nine-hour round which breaks down to only a half an hour per hole is perfectly reasonable. But this foursome will not permit any other members to play through them. We have spoken to them, written to them, pleaded with them. On occasion we will send a brace of caddies ahead to ask if we can play through. These caddies are cursed, abused, and often beaten.

For the past few weeks we have, in trying to combat this absurd problem, scheduled a number of tournaments. One was for the Westchester Open and we engaged over thirty of the nation's top professionals. A large gallery was present and the teeing-off schedule worked fine from eight o'clock to nine. But promptly at nine the foursome appeared. Their caddies were armed with quarter whips and they wedged themselves and the foursome through the crowd and onto the tee. Needless to say this important professional tournament was postponed and eventually called off. The audience was reimbursed and the professionals were enraged.

The Greens Committee meets again in three weeks and the main problem on the agenda is the foursome. We would appreciate any comments.

CHARLES Q. GRIGG
Ardsley, N. Y.

Dear Sir,

In one sentence you mention you are proud of your adherence to Eagle-Ho standards. Later on you state you are conducting a professional tournament and that the professionals were enraged.

Sir, how can this be? Are you so unfamiliar with

Eagle-Ho as to acknowledge a professional, much less discuss a professional's emotional problems?

I choose to think you are jesting. In the unlikely event you are not, your club will immediately be taken from the Eagle-Ho roll.

As to the problem of the slow foursome, I will refrain from any comment until I hear from you regarding the defection. Kindly refer to Eagle-Ho Encyclopedia No. 2, under Professionals—Their Non-existence. I expect to hear from you within the next ten days.

As ever,
Dr. Golf

73.

Dear Doctor Golf,

Is it true that you have recognized a number of Benedictine monasteries and their courses as Eagle-Ho?

Monsignor Guillaume
New Haven, Conn.

Dear Sir,

It is partly true, sir. While many have tried to qualify, and I must hastily admit that those attempting to qualify have progressed mightily, only two Orders in this country and one in France have been awarded full Eagle-Ho privileges.

Last year I visited France and played in the annual tournament on the Eve of the Nativity of St. James the Less, and I have never played with a more enthusiastic or wholesome group of golfers in a long, long time. I must also tell you that the Benedictines are doing absolutely marvelous things with a new hybrid of Bermuda grass suitable for areas above the seventy-degree parallel.

As ever,
Dr. Golf

74.

Dear Doctor Golf,

During the past three years I have been under a doctor's counsel as to food, sleep, exercise, etc. He claims that an all-protein diet with lettuce and milk, vigorous exercise upon getting up, and no more than seven hours' sleep is the ideal plan for me.

He also predicted that my golf game would improve. I have followed this man's advice to the letter, but unfortunately my game gets worse. My woods are weak and short, my irons dull and listless, and my approaches and putts are completely lacking in authority. Five years ago I played to a Florida Golf Association Handicap of 3, three years ago it was 5. Now it is 10 and tomorrow it may well be 14. Is there some way I can stop this deterioration?

B. Heatter
Rivo Alto, Fla.

Dear Sir,

Back in 1894 one of my father's students here at Eagle-Ho was the Reverend Timothy Titcomb. It would, I feel, be impossible for me to answer your letter any better than Reverend Titcomb has done almost seventy years ago. I quote:

It is a hard sight to see a young man with the pluck all taken out of him by a meagre diet, his whole nature starved, degenerated, emasculated. An Englishman cannot fight without beef in his belly; no more can a man thrive on theories and milk. Plank beds, brief sleep and early walks will come to nought.

If Ben Franklin ever originated the maxim "Six hours of sleep for a man, seven hours for a woman and eight for a fool," he ought uniformly to have practiced by the rule of the last number.

If some fanatic has made you believe that it is good for you to be violently wakened from your sleep at an early hour, and to go out into the damp raw air, morning after morning with your fast unbroken and your body unfortified by the stimulus of food, forget him and his counsels and take full measure of your rest.

Here ends the letter of the Reverend Timothy Titcomb.

As ever,
Dr. Golf

75.

Dear Doctor Golf,

My husband, who is 35 years old and rather tall, has been gone for seven years. He left me with four children and his ailing parents, along with a number of his old golf debts. I have held two jobs ever since he left and I am managing to get the children through school and the debts paid off. I now have every reason to believe he is staying at your Eagle-Ho Camp. Enclosed is his photograph as I am sure he has changed his name.

Julia Worm
Rochester, N. Y.

My dear Mrs. Worm,

Eagle-Ho is *not* a camp. Eagle-Ho is a sanctuary and in no sense can it be considered a camp, a spa, or any other recreation reserve.

If you have occasion to write us again I must insist that you use the proper name—Eagle-Ho Sanctuary.

As ever,
DR. GOLF

76.

Dear Doctor Golf,

The other night at a party a golfing friend told us that you are still making clubs with wooden shafts. We have placed a rather sizable bet stating that this couldn't be. Would you please advise us at your earliest convenience.

GREENS COMMITTEE
Winged Foot Country Club
Rye, N. Y.

Gentlemen:

My grandfather in Scotland, my father here at Eagle-Ho and I, sir, have always, and will always, use wooden shafts on all Eagle-Ho clubs. In the unlikely event that iron, steel or some composition material ever proves satisfactory I would instantly forbid its use on any and all Eagle-Ho approved courses. How could a golfer play with anything but a wooden shafted club? How could a true golfer know his clubs if the shafts were made of some material other than wood? Could a man know a stone, a piece of brass, a block of ice? With a wooden shaft one feels the club and the ball.

The esthetics alone: the grain, the proper wax, the stain, the smooth clear varnish—what is there that could replace this magic? I sir, say, Nothing!

Occasionally I will flex a shaft and think on the men before me—Ray, Vardon, the incomparable Travis—and I know that the path they trod was the right one and as long as there is breath in my body and blood in my veins I will continue to follow these golden examples.

As ever,
DR. GOLF

77.

Dear Doctor Golf,

I have received a letter and a postal from you recently. Both were worded as if to a truant child, condescending and polemical. Is there always this almost unbearable attitude of superiority in your messages?

TADEUSZ GOLAS
Paterson, N. J.

Dear Sir,

I do not write to be read by all people nor do I write to be read by all golfers. I write as I would speak to my members, my students, and my friends here at Eagle-Ho.

If you find this offensive I cannot truly say I am sorry. A man lives by his style: style, in short, is the man. My style is the way I am and if you choose to dislike it I am afraid that is a problem I would have to decline solving.

I would like to add that if you detect an air of superiority it is only that which I find necessary for describing the experiences and the truth which my heart holds.

As ever,
DR. GOLF

78.

Dear Doctor Golf,

Out here in Long Island we have a public course called Bethpage. It has six courses, and the most famous is the difficult Black Course, I hear. Sam

Snead has rated it as one of the toughest courses in the world. I was wondering if you have ever played it.
WILLIAM FOLLEN
Mineola, N. Y.

Dear Sir,

I have never played on any public golf course. Who is Sam Snead?   As ever,
DR. GOLF

79.

Dear Doctor Golf,

I read somewhere that in the early days of golf, caddies acted as procurers of women for the members Often teas, parties, orgies would occur on the links and the caddies would socialize, solicit and obtain favors for their masters. Would you comment on this.
EVELYN STUART, ESQ.
Tuscany, Ga.

Dear Sir,

This did happen, sir, in Scotland, later in England, at Carnoustie, Glen Eagles, St. Andrews. At all times, however, the master and caddy relationship was rigidly adhered to. If you will study the old prints you will note that the caddies are serving the Lairds and their Ladies. Often they, the caddies, would act as jesters and perform little comic acts, but always there were menservants and runners of messages. The practice of flogging, the use of stocks, quarter whips, and immersion flourished in these halcyon days.

Often I think how sad it is that we have been unable to preserve so little of this time, this grand manner, and how we have been forced into a limp, watery form of golf that Bonnie Prince Charles would have found unrecognizable.

Perhaps the greatest defection from the Royal and Ancient Code occurred in this country not too many years back. It was, and I shudder to write, the odious and reprehensible creation and acceptance of the professional. This great stride into the darkness was started by that upstart, young Jordan, at the Country Club in Brookline. Prior to this, professionals were kept in their place. Their place was next to the caddy. Since he was no more than an extension of the caddy, and usually without a caddy's good manners, his lodging and meals were taken at the Caddy House. But with Jordan's ascendancy the professional began appearing in the club house itself. The U.S.G.A. and P.G.A. have encouraged this foul thing. Long have I reproached them for this madness, but with little or no success.

At Eagle-Ho approved clubs I allow no fraternization between professional and member. The professional is required to wear the same livery as caddies and doormen. He is not beyond flogging or the stocks. I have made only one concession to this band of brigands in the past forty years and that is the rescinding of the Edict of Augusta on immersions. Professionals at Eagle-Ho approved clubs may not be immersed unless it is by a unanimous decision of the Greens Committee.

As ever,
Dr. Golf

80.

Dear Doctor Golf,

I have been studying your book "Golf for Stout People" for four years. It has been very helpful until recently. I am 5 feet 7 and I now weigh 270 pounds.

While I have large shoulders, arms, and hands, unfortunately most of my weight is in my stomach.

Following your advice to stout people I have opened my stance to correct this and allowed my hips and hands to enter the shot. I now find I can open my stance more only by standing 90 degrees to the direction of intended flight of the ball. Is there some way I can avoid this awkward and unsatisfactory method other than by severe, and possibly debilitating dieting?

GEORGE DIETRICH
Montgomery, Ala.

Dear Sir,

If I may have a picture of you in profile I believe I will be able to help. Often in cases like yours we find that the stomach, if properly developed, can be substituted for the hips. In other words, instead of rotating hips to bring in the power and allow arms and hands to enter the shot, one merely rotates the stomach. On the surface this may seem like an easy remedy. It is not. You will need coaching, diagrams, and apparatuses, but if you pursue this method seriously I see no reason why you cannot eventually enjoy a normal stance.

As ever,
DR. GOLF

81.

Dear Doctor Golf,

What provisions, if any, are made at Eagle-Ho Sanctuary for men who have distinguished themselves in Eagle-Ho golf and then passed on?

WILLIAM GREELEY
Sacramento, Calif.

Dear Sir,

I have mentioned at some time in my letters the vast entrance to Eagle-Ho. This entrance was inspired by Blenheim Castle in England and has the same large and magnificent hallway. In this hallway is the history of Eagle-Ho golf. As one enters one is immediately aware of the shrinelike quality that pervades the historic sanctuary. On the left the bust of Travis reigns. There are casts of great swings, death masks of the great Scots, and sculptured bronzes of classic grips. Panoramic murals showing famous shots are to the right, and beneath these are the glass cases containing autographed balls, golf gloves, and shoes. Vardon's driver, Ray's mashie, and Travis's niblick are under glass on the far wall, and rising to the ceiling is the bronze list of members—their date of birth, date of acceptance in Eagle-Ho, their date of death, and their list of eagles.   As ever,
                                              Dr. Golf

82.

Dear Doctor Golf,

At our club five years ago we adopted the U.S.G.A. ruling of penalizing a player two strokes for out of bounds. Two years ago this ruling was changed to one stroke, and now it is back at two strokes. Is there any indication that this ruling will be rescinded and the penalty will again be one stroke?

                              F. Fulgence Bartlett
                              Lancaster, Pa.

Dear Sir,

If you have any questions on U.S.G.A. proceedings I suggest you direct such inquiries to them. By now you should realize that the U.S.G.A. and the P.G.A. are heretical schisms that have departed from the historic rules of St. Andrews and the tenets of Eagle-Ho. At Eagle-Ho we recognize the U.S.G.A. in some areas; the P.G.A. in none.

My Edict of Atlanta, the Council of Baltusrol, and the denunciation and expulsion of Jordan clearly spell out our firm stand here at Eagle-Ho. There have been several councils engineered by the U.S.G.A. to bring us closer together. In every case—the last one was the Council of Monterey—the U.S.G.A. was interested in my recognizing the P.G.A. Since I have never, and will never, recognize any P.G.A. members, I refused to listen to appeals of mollification.

My stand is simple. I do not tolerate any commercial or mercenary influence on Eagle-Ho rulings; the U.S.G.A. does. Every public whim, every commercial pressure is felt and reflected in its constantly changing rules. There are three powers in golf: the Scottish, Eagle-Ho, and the U.S.G.A. If you know your history of golf you should be aware of the fact that Scottish and Eagle-Ho rulings are irrefutable and all decisions on policy and interpretations are infallible. An answer as to what U.S.G.A. may rule next year on out-of-bounds is impossible. If they follow their shaky and vacillating policies of the past we may well find the ruling three strokes, four strokes, five strokes. It may even be no strokes.   As ever,

DR. GOLF

83.

Dear Doctor Golf,

What is your opinion of the low state of dress on golf courses of America?   PHILIP W. DRAKE
Short Hills, N. J.

Dear Sir,

It is at a stage now, sir, where it can get no worse.
I see yellows, reds, greens abounding in trousers,
multicolor shoes and harlequin stockings, and all
manner of sweaters and umbrellas. It has gone far too
far, and these obstreperous idiots—these so-called
professionals—are reaping the seeds of their folly by
encouraging and attracting absolutely the lowest type
of people into golf. Clerks, men in trade, plumbers,
bricklayers, sellers of pork, glaziers of glass, taper
makers—the list rises and soars into absolute incred-
ibility. Most of the blame can be laid at the feet of
the U.S.G.A.: their democratic process, their mon-
strous and absurd belief in the common man, their
encouragement of miniature golf, golf for women,
driving ranges, three-hole golf courses, etc., etc., etc.
But another side to this insidious wedge that is driving the quality down is the flamboyantly dressed
teaching professional and the orange-trousered fools
that pass themselves off as touring professionals.

I say study the masters. Study the old prints and
study them carefully. Do you see these excesses? No!
Rich clothes, like loud clothes, are a sign of mental
poverty. A rich but modest cravat sustaining a fault-
less dickey is about the limit of elegance among the
greats. Browns, buffs, and similar earth colors are the
basic colors at Eagle-Ho and nowhere does one see
shirt sleeves or uncovered arms. One rule I insist on
is that a vest should be worn at all times and that
while it should harmonize, it could be of some
muted color and all robing should be shaded off from
it until there is not an obtrusive feature.

I am afraid I can say no more without getting
too emotional. Mr. Drake, golf is in grave danger
in this country if these excesses are permitted to
flourish.   As ever,

DR. GOLF

84.

Dear Doctor Golf,

I have been playing golf with the same partner for over forty years. In the club house before the round, in the club house after the round, you would never meet a more cheerful, outgoing, friendly, enthusiastic friend. However, once we reach the first tee and until we hole out on the 18th green he doesn't say a word. He walks alone, he stands alone, and when any conversation is required he merely nods at the caddy who in turn speaks for him.

Can you, sir, give me some advice on how to solve this perplexing problem?

GEORGE GORMAN
Yonkers, N. Y.

Dear Sir,

I have read your letter very carefully. Precisely what is your problem?

As ever,
DR. GOLF

85.

Dear Doctor Golf,

Is there a plaque over the door at Eagle-Ho Sanctuary? If so, what does it say?

Yours Very Truly,
W. H. MANVILLE
Des Moines, Iowa

Dear Sir,

Yes, we have a plaque at Eagle-Ho over our main entrance. It is between the bust of Travis and the panoramic mural of Glen Eagles. The plaque is bronze and on it are enscribed the immortal words of Henry Leach:

Men who were innocent and have turned to golf do not give a reason why: they are silent to the questioner. They say that he too will see in time, and then they golf exceedingly.

As ever,
DR. GOLF

86.

Dear Doctor Golf,

There is a book around called "Psychological Golf" by a J. H. Clarke, Ph.D. It is selling for $7.50 and all my friends tell me it is very good. I was wondering if you have read it and, if so, what was your reaction.

BUD COBURN
Louisville, Ky.

Dear Sir,

My first action was to have the book immediately indexed. The author is essentially a psychologist, and his province, while questionable, is an interesting one, but he presumes a good deal on the good nature and/or ignorance of his audience when he attempts to talk about the real things that happen in golf.

He bills himself as a dedicated amateur, whatever that is supposed to mean. I have checked my files and friends and the question kept recurring, "Sir, who are you?"

He is neither Eagle-Ho or U.S.G.A. He is unknown in Scotland and has no rank in the long list of international amateurs.

I have always frowned on terms such as "the psychological approach," "frustration-free," "application of psychological principles," and in this book they abound. They are silken clothes elaborately arranged over a festering dunghill of ignorance and commercial depravity.

Do not buy this book. Do not buy it or give it as a gift and, if it is at all possible, convince your friends it will sow confusion and chaos where now there is some measure of content.

The book, in short, sir, is a dismal and melancholy attempt to make money.

As ever,
Dr. Golf

87.

Dear Dr. Golf:

Although I have only a nodding acquaintance with your game, I am familiar with your writings, and respect them. You are obviously a professional in your field in the very best sense of that much maligned word. To cast modesty to the winds, I, too, can lay some claim to professionalism in my field, which is angling for the trout in fast water by means of the dry fly.

I was musing the other evening about some of the common touchstones, the symbolic parallels that may be said to obtain between our sports. You hold a club, I wave a wand. You are faced with the necessity of making accurate putts over treacherous ground into a small hole; I confront the delicate situation of placing my fly in the right place, in the right manner so as to float it over a wary and experienced fish. Although your hole does not move, and my fish might take fright and dart away, I have noted a number of psychological parallels between golfers and fishermen —their intensity, their calm under pressure, the tendency to exaggeration or displays of temper running in inverse ratio to their ability. Do you fish yourself? (I somehow feel you must.)

By the way, I have access to a stretch of the Lower Neversink that I believe you would truly appreciate. After reading of your lovely courses in Arkansas, I sometimes think of it as the trout fisherman's Eagle-Ho. Perhaps next May, when the Blue Duns are emerging, you might grant me the pleasure of your company.   Sincerely,
NICHOLAS BRECKENRIDGE II
Horseheads, N. Y.

Dear Sir,

Son, my mother's name was Breckenridge. I was raised in your part of the country, and as a lad I well remember your grandfather and your father. Many times have I fished with the elder Breckenridge—the Onondaga, the Oswegatchie, the fiery Canajoharie itself. These were happy days. These were marvelous days. How clearly I recall your father and the grace and beauty of his classic movement. The pure unhurried line. He had no flourishes, no gimmicks that made it look harder or better. It was—and is, I am sure, to this day—pure, lean, classic, indeed superlative. His cast rose of its ownself into a perfectly balanced parabola. How well I recall it all. . . .

Smooth and low and almost motionless at the bottom, rising gradually as if controlled by some phantom breeze in the center and arching down or stretching out as far as the farthest dark pool or as near as the nearest sun-flecked bed.

So you are Nicholas Breckenridge's son?

Often at Eagle-Ho I get a patient who due to some psychic block or traumatic experience is unable to hold a club, address a ball, or even look down the fairway. Whenever this happens I lead this confused but gentle soul to one of our many streams and there I try to teach him what your grandfather taught me. The confidence, the rhythm, together with the tranquil setting often works wonders and soon this man is once again back on the fairways at Eagle-Ho.

Yes, my boy, there is a relation between fly casting and golf. It is the calmness and the detachment that comes after one truly knows the art. Perhaps it can be compared to the mystic's idea of ascension, that rare moment when the mind and body join as one and are free of all encumbrance, and receptivity begins. I have seen this look of grace and beatitude on few men's faces in my time. I have seen it in the faces of my friends here at Eagle-Ho and on your grandfather's patrician brow as he fished the Onondaga. No other art form, save music, elicits this rare and tender compassion.

As ever,
DR. GOLF

88.

Dear Dr. Golf,

As a youth I played baseball, football, basketball, and tennis, and, judging from the mantelpiece filled with silver goblets and inscribed punch bowls, I must admit I played well. I have always assumed that golf would be an easy game to take up when I got older. Now I am thirty-five and find I cannot play the rigorous games of yesterday. I have watched the players at the driving range and occasionally I will try my hand at driving. It appears to be an easy and amusing game. I was wondering if you could give me any basic pointers as I don't want to waste much time getting into the game.

> I remain,
> KNOX BURGER
> The Arsenal,
> Harper's Ferry, Va.

Dear Sir,

Indeed it would be amusing but not for long, for soon you would see the depth of your folly. Football, baseball, basketball—my dear sir, you have virtually frittered away your athletic patrimony.

Someone with an ignorance and the lack of respect for golf that approaches yours once remarked how middle age brought golf rather than wisdom. This poverty of the understanding is much like yours. I am returning your letter with the advice that if you are seeking to begin golf at this late stage in your life with the idea that the game is amusing I would suggest you look elsewhere.

> As ever,
> DR. GOLF

89.

Dear Doctor Golf,

You probably don't remember me. I just spent some time at Doctor Golf Eagle-Ho Sanctuary at Eagle-Ho, Arkansas. You diagnosed my case as "a pernicious psychic indifference resulting in an inability to get any power into my shots." I was in the isolation ward for over four months. I didn't like the lectures on the Rosicrucians and all those therapeutic baths at first, but after a while I got so I didn't mind them. I still get a lot of mail from the Rosicrucians who, by the way, turned out to be a swell bunch of fellows.

Things aren't quite the same at home; I guess you didn't know that. My wife remarried and my kids are all in high school. The boy is using my second set of Eagle-Ho clubs and it looks like he's got a lot of natural talent. Oh, yes, my leave of absence from my job to attend Eagle-Ho didn't quite cover the 3½ years I was gone.

The game is great now. I'm long off the tee and I'm getting that little tail end hook you showed me. The wife took most of the furniture when she left. I smashed out three walls, the living room, dining room and kitchen, and I can now use the driver in the house.

My putting has really come alive with your Eagle-Ho velvet-faced model when the weather's dry. It don't do so good when it's damp because the ball dwells too long on the face. Sometimes it even sticks. But on dry days when it's hot it's really wonderful.

I guess you want to know why I'm writing? Well, it's like this. Like I said the wife and the kids have been gone and they took the radio and TV set and I've been practicing driving from the front room

to the back kitchen wall. Well, it's been getting cool lately and I had some estimates and it comes out pretty expensive. Now the way I got it figured, I could add another $1,000 to the estimate and I could afford a winter and spring at Eagle-Ho Sanctuary. I figure if I could get a little more distance off the tee I'd be in great shape. I figure I could leave Eagle-Ho, say, around March and maybe pick up the winter circuit when it hits Louisiana.

But, Doctor, I don't believe I could stand another winter of those therapeutic baths. They were nice and all that and I got so after a while that I liked the attendants. But a lot of times that water wasn't too warm and you know how long they like to lock you in.

Now I'm not complaining. Don't get that idea. But you know yourself the damage that too much bathing can do to your hands. I got these nice calluses now and I figure if I get locked in that bath for twelve hours or so they'll get too soft and tender.

So here's my proposition. If you'll send me a note stating no baths, no Rosicrucian lectures, no shock treatment, I'll mail you a check for $4,000 to cover the winter and spring season.

> Obediently yours,
> ROBERT CONWAY
> Rye, N. Y.

Dear Mr. Conway,

We have far, far too many applicants who are perfectly willing to abide by the procedure and policy of Eagle-Ho to make any exceptions. I have studied your case rather thoroughly and I find that baths are a part of your program that could not be circumvented. I am sorry, Mr. Conway, we will have to turn your application for Eagle-Ho Sanctuary down this year.

Mr. Conway, when you left us this last spring we noticed a rather large number of towels and silver missing. Would you be so kind as to check your luggage and if the articles have been inadvertently packed we would appreciate your returning them.

> Yours,
> DR. GOLF

90.

Dear Doctor Golf,

Throughout your letters and lectures I notice you never recommend using a wedge from the sand traps. Do you recommend a putter for all sand shots. . . . ?

HARVEY PINGER
Mont Bliss, Idaho

Dear Mr. Pinger,

By now you know that I am of the old school. In short, I deplore the use of any form of wedge. It's unsightly, unbalanced, not regulation, and not in keeping with the high standards of golf. Ted Ray, Harry Vardon, Walter Hagen used no wedge, why should I; and for that matter why should you?

Stick with your putter, Mr. Pinger. It's your best friend. And the confidence you gain with it in the sand traps—be they shallow, deep, lipped or unlipped —can be psychologically transferred onto the green. Anyone can play a wedge out of the sand trap just as anybody can hit driving-range wood shots. But the skill, the dexterity, the coordination required to master the putter out of the deep sand is a quality that, once achieved, you will always cherish and your opponents will forever envy.

If you find you are having undue difficulty, check the putter shaft. If you are using a stiff shaft the chances are that is your problem. I recommend a soft flexible shaft and a thin-bladed upright putter face. Check your stance. Be sure you are digging in. And, most important, be sure that the club face is wide open.

As ever,
DR. GOLF

91.

Dear Doctor Golf,

I have been on the Dyker Beach Club waiting list for seventeen years. I am a devoted reader and have bought over two hundred of your books, plus many of your swing control guides and power mechanisms.

I watch All-Star Golf on the television and practice every night on your 36-Hole 4-Room Wall-to-Wall Rug. I think I am ready now. I realize you would be jeopardizing your position with the U.S.G.A., but I wish you would mention my name to the membership committee.

PEER PEDERSEN
Rye, N. Y.

Dear Mr. Pedersen,

You are in luck. The other night I met the president of the Admissions Committee, the chairman of the Golf Committee, and two prominent members of Dyker Beach. I have turned over your letter to them with my enthusiastic recommendation for your immediate membership. They all agreed that you are ready for membership and asked me to pass on their apologies for this lengthy wait. You can expect a letter from the committee very soon now.

I have many memories of Dyker Beach. They have an excellent marina and superb chef. I am sure you will be happy there. Incidentally, as you enter the club-house door look to your right. There's a bronze plaque commemorating my Walker Cup victory.

As ever,
DR. GOLF

P.S. You're in luck again! I see by the records that your house has two 220-volt outlets. My new Spring and Swing Eagle-Ho muscle toner equipment is now ready. I have been using it myself lately and it's really terrific for building up power in the small of your back. You still have a credit of $606.11. The retail price for the Spring and Swing Eagle-Ho complete with leather straps, giant coil springs, wall and floor protective mats, and a full-phase 95-horsepower Pratt & Whitney motor is $829.16. I am shipping the Eagle-Ho unit prepaid this week. This will bring your outstanding balance to $223.05. Good luck at Dyker Beach.

92.

Dear Dr. Golf,

Many of the players there at the Rolling Mead Country Club stretch the winter ruling to the absolute limit. Often they will kick the earth fiercely with their heel and then place the ball on the raised portion of the ground. Sometimes this raised portion is four or five inches high. As you can see, when this is done what might have been a close iron lie on the fairway now becomes an easy wood position. I am confident that the U.S.G.A. has outlawed this practice, but I am unable to find the exact ruling. Dr. Golf, where in the U.S.G.A. discussion of winter rulings can I find this point discussed?

JAMES THOMPSON
Florence, S. C.

Dear Sir,

I am sure that if you continue searching the U.S.G.A. statutes of limitations regarding winter rulings you will find the proper addendum covering your particular problem. I have not chosen to familiarize myself with any phase of the so-called winter rulings because I have never recognized this ridiculous practice. For a long time I actively fought the U.S.G.A. on this, but their loud cries for lenity and understanding for northern golfers, golfers playing on new and immature courses, and golfers playing on courses where roads and houses were being erected sickened me and I withdrew. At Eagle-Ho and on all Eagle-Ho courses around the world we do not recognize any tempering of the basic Eagle-Ho rulings. In short, sir, golf knows no season, no climate and no geography . . . golf, sir, as in life itself, is played as the ball lies.

As ever,
Dr. Golf

93.

Dear Dr. Golf,

I am wondering if you recognize the National Amateur Golf Tournament?

George Dean
Winston-Salem, N. C.

Dear Sir,

The National Amateur, the Invitational at The National Links in Southampton, a handful of amateur tournaments, and that portion of the Masters that is amateur are heartily recognized here at Eagle-Ho. I do not recognize any professional tournament nor do I recognize any caddy tournament. The moment money enters into a tournament the calibre of the players, and the gallery, distends to a crass, commercial mediocrity that I find intolerable. A laurel wreath, a set of wood covers, a piece of engraved silver is more than sufficient for a winner. The modern prizes of $1,000 and more have nurtured and spawned the blight that is now upon the fairways and the greens of this country.

As ever,
DR. GOLF

94.

Dear Dr. Golf,

I cannot get distance on my drives. I have followed all of your instructions about knee locking, hip rotation, super pronation, and every shot is finished, as you prescribe, at the soft spot under the base of my right ear. Still I don't get the distance I need. On a flat, untrapped 350-yard hole I need to hit a brassie second shot and usually this is followed by a rather long niblick shot to the green. Dr. Golf, how can I get a longer ball off the tee?

Very truly yours,
KURT VONNEGUT
Barnstable, Mass.

Dear Sir,

A brassie second shot plus a niblick third shot obviously means you are not getting the length you need off the tee. I believe we should now try imparting maximum overspin to your driving shot. This overspin will keep the ball low and it will give you a much longer ball than you are now realizing. Basically, I want you to think in terms of closing the driver face and snatching up at the point of impact. Do not attempt one without the other—let me repeat this—do not attempt one without the other, for the effect is disastrous. A closed face will result in a violent hook into the whins and kelp, while a snatched shot will produce the worst variety of the uncontrolled scull. But a properly executed closed face and snatch will give you a low, beautiful, spinning shot that is a joy to watch. The shot never rises as does the shot that is pinched (enclosed is my letter to Mr. McDermott on the use of the Baffy-Spoon and instructions for the Flag Shot), but remains approximately 6 to 8 feet above the ground. If the shot strikes a rise in the fairway or a bunker top the maximum overspin takes over and the ball fairly leaps back into the air and hurtles itself toward the green.

Do not change your swing, your knee lock, your degree of super pronation, or your finish. All this remains as it is, but to this you must now add the closed face and the rapid snatching. Since these two ingredients can be effectively introduced within the 8 inches of your hitting area, there is no reason to change any part of your Eagle-Ho swing. . . . Soon, on short holes, you will be able to cast out the brassie second shot as you would a noxious serpent.

As ever,
DR. GOLF

95.

Dear Dr. Golf,

Who, in your opinion, are the great golfers of our present day?

JAMES WALLACE
Greater Los Angeles, Calif.

Dear Sir,

I have covered this subject more than adequately in several letters in the past, but since you choose to ignore or forget them I will, for the last time, state my convictions. It is my judgment that, with the possible exception of Chick Evans and Robert Jones and the upstart young Jordan, we have had no golfers in this country since Walter Travis.

While today's so-called modern professional can win as much as three and even four thousand dollars in a single year's play this in no way means he is a golfer. He is, in short, a tradesman and in no wit differs from the mattress renovators and the sellers of port that clog the carriages of modern business today.

Sir Franklin Remington-Lee of Scotland summed up my sentiment when he so eloquently proclaimed at the funeral of Tom Morris the Elder, "Où sont les golfeurs d'antan?"

As ever,
Dr. Golf

96.

Dear Dr. Golf,

We are the largest manufacturer of golf tees in the world. Some of our firsts have been the plastic Day-Glo tee, the magnetic tee which can be picked up with the heel of the club, the extra-long and extra-short tee, and the extremely successful two-inch plastic tee in the form of a lifelike forty-inch-bosomed bathing beauty.

We are aware of the fact that you do not buy golf tees, but we were wondering if we could interest you in a rather unique idea at this time. Our artists and sculptors have come up with a new approach to

tees that I am confident you will be pleased with. We
have taken the liberty to create, design, and render
the enclosed two-inch reproductions of the tees we
have in mind. Model A is an exact reproduction of
Eagle-Ho Sanctuary. We believe the best color here
would be white. Model B is an attempt to render your
image. Since photographs of you are unavailable we
used one of our own models. You will note how we
achieve the conclavity in the head for receiving the
ball without any noticeable loss of dignity in the
image itself. We are very proud of this submission,
and we hope you will favor us with an order. Bro-
chures and prices are attached.

HUBERT JOHNSON,
Par Flight Tee and Golf Novelty Co.
Brooklyn, N. Y.

Dear Sir,

What a low and worthless profession you have chosen! You should be flogged and driven from the land.

All of the tees you enclosed were completely without merit, but the small statue of the unfrocked young lady scraped the very bottom of your barrel of obscenities. I have instructed my wireless operators to notify all Eagle-Ho clubs to make a determined effort to publish my contempt for your company and your vile products on all the golfing billboards of the world.

The wooden, the plastic, the metal tee—for that matter, any rigid tee—is as ridiculous and as unsightly as the multicolored umbrellas and the zippered bags that befoul the fairways of America. For your further —and final—information, at Eagle-Ho we still use and shall continue to use the original tee of Bonnie Prince Charles, that being the small cone of sand artfully placed by hand on the driving tee.

DR. GOLF

97.

Dear Dr. Golf,

I am doing a book for the University of Chicago Press showing that golf is a highly developed substitute for sex. No doubt you are aware of the continual references in Sigmund Freud's work to the male and female symbols underlying all games. It is my contention that in golf we reach the absolute zenith in this psychodrama.

On the masculine side we find: sticks, balls, clubs, doglegs, etc. On the distaff side: bunkers, traps, aprons, holes, cups, etc. The metaphysical poets have

compared fairways and the rolling greens to a woman's form; while the boldness and authority from the tee and on the long iron shots, coupled with the dexterity on the apron and the finesse around the cup, is too obvious for discussion. Even the caddy who removes the stick from the cup, finds the balls, carries the bag (guilt) plays an important role. Can the word caddy not be traced back and be seen to be an obvious attempt to conceal and yet use the word "Daddy"? Also the camaraderie in the locker room, the jostling in the shower, the snapping of towels, the appearance of the "buddy system," the almost unanimous chorus of "He's in the shower" whenever one of the players is summoned (threatened) by wife, fiancée or mother—these are only a few of my theories based on Freud's work. The rest you can read at your leisure when the book is published. The title is GOLF . . . A CONQUEST OF SEX.

M. ALLEN
University of Chicago

Dear Mr. Allen,

Possibly your Mr. Freud, like so many other malcontents, resented golf for the simple reason he could not play. Perhaps he was unable to get into the country club of his choosing. I am unfamiliar with his psychology, as I am unfamiliar with a number of other pseudosciences that flash across our fraud-ridden intellectual firmament. Psychology, like sociology and economics, is at best a dismal science producing nothing save its own vocabulary and a comfortable living for its leaders. Mr. Sigmund Freud sounds like he, too—being unable to excel in golf or any other outdoor sport—has dedicated his work to an abortive attempt to render golf meaningless to others . . . possibly he also suffers from a dirty mind.

Vardon, Travis, Ted Ray, Tom Morris the Elder will be remembered long after your Mr. Freud's books and ideas have passed on and vanished . . . I can say no more.

As ever,
DR. GOLF

98.

Dear Dr. Golf,

Was Kenneth Grahame, the author of "The
Wind in the Willows," a friend of your father's?
I would also like to know if Mr. Grahame ever
visited this country.

Sincerely yours,
MISS SARAH WILSON CRAWFORD
San Francisco, Calif.

Dear Miss Crawford,

Kenneth Grahame, Theodore Roosevelt, the
Earl of Wight, and my father played many rounds
at Eagle-Ho in Scotland. Unfortunately, Mr.
Grahame did not visit these shores, despite the many
invitations from my father and Mr. Roosevelt. You
may be interested in learning that Mr. E. H. Sheppard's sketches of "Toad Hall" in "The Wind in the
Willows" for Mr. Grahame were inspired by the
towers and battlements of Eagle-Ho in Scotland.

It was my pleasure to have followed this illustri-
ous foursome many times, and I can report that Mr.
Grahame had the makings of a first-rate golfer. Unfortunately, he was given to wandering near the
banks of streams and staring into badger and mole
holes and thus slowed the play down immeasurably.
How often have I watched the massive Roosevelt
upbraid him for this folly and then slap him stoutly
on the back and push him forward to the next shot.
In the end, however, Mr. Grahame prevailed, for
who can deny that "Toad" of "Toad Hall" is not
the perfectly rendered caricature of the Honorable
Teddy Roosevelt. . . .

As ever,
DR. GOLF

99.

Dear Dr. Golf,

   Since you deprecate the "dying ball" for putting as well as the bold shot for the back of the cup I was wondering what possible shot you recommend for putting?

I remain,
ROBERT WEIR
St. Louis, Mo.

Dear Sir,

   The "dying ball" and the "bold putt" enjoy a brief vogue every decade or so, and being of easy comprehension they are usually encouraged by journalists and fools. But the limitations of these shots cannot be concealed for long and soon they pass from sight.

   At Eagle-Ho I teach the "spinning putt," which long since has been scientifically proven to be superior to any and all putting shots. The "basic swing for the spinning putt" has been discussed in my letter on "Putter Dwell." Briefly, the spinning putt is caused to rotate clockwise by a dragging of the club head at impact from right to left. The ball is aimed firmly and slightly to the left of the hole. Confidence and aggressiveness in striking this shot are mandatory, and when it is done properly the results are amazing. The spinning ball from left to right will actually search out and find the hole, and if the slightest edge of the ball touches the hole the action will pull the ball in and down. Unlike the "dying ball" which like its name usually dies short of the hole and the "bold putt" which can on fast greens leap from the very green itself, the spinning putt busies itself with searching out the hole and dropping in. This putt is especially good on rolling greens where firm control is needed.

As ever,

DR. GOLF

100.

Dear Dr. Golf,

Thanks to you I am now a full-fledged member of the Dyker Beach Country Club. Three weeks ago today I was notified of my acceptance. If you will recall I had been on the waiting list for over seventeen years. The club membership is considerably larger than I thought it would be. As near as I can estimate, the membership is between six and seven thousand members, but they seem to be a nice bunch and so far I have had a marvelous time. I haven't played much golf so far, since most of the time here has been spent in standing on line. I met Harry Kraus here two weeks ago, he is a bacon salesman from Lefrak City. He held my place on line while I went out to the grassy area in the middle of Atlantic Ave. and took some practice swings. We aren't allowed to take practice swings on line, and since the entire area between the club house and the first tee is concrete I don't like to swing my Eagle-Ho clubs and take any risk of chipping them.

Harry and I played last week with a woman gynecologist and an Indian who is in this country lobbying for the cashew nut interests. It was the lady doctor's first round of golf and we sure had fun watching her. Harry counted all of her strokes and her total score for 18 holes was 346. The Indian played badly. I guess it was because he was wearing

all of those robes. Harry didn't keep his score. Anyhow, after it was over we went inside the club house and had knishes and Dr. Brown's Celery Soda and spent about an hour or so telling funny golf stories. Oh, I looked for the plaque dedicated to you on the wall, but the only sign I saw was from the Fire Dept. stating that it was against the law to have over 900 in the room at one time. There was an interesting sign in the men's room under the Beware Pickpockets announcement—it read *Do Not Use Toilet Tissue to Dry Hands* . . . I don't know why anyone would want to use it, because next to every fourth washstand is one of those little electric hand dryer units.

You also mentioned the wood panels in the club house and the chef. The wood panels have been replaced by white tile; it's the same kind you see in the subways. I understand this makes the place easier to clean and also it is easy to break up mob scenes. They do something with ammonia and water.

I went inside the kitchen to pay your respects to the chef. The cook inside began to laugh and kept pointing toward New York City. I think he said something about the chef now being at the Pavillon. . . .

On your next visit to New York maybe you could play along with Harry and me.

Yours truly,
PEER PEDERSEN
Rye, N. Y.

Dear Sir,

We must be talking about two different courses.
As ever,
DR. GOLF

101.

Dear Dr. Golf,

I have a patient who has also been my golfing partner for fifteen years. Last year at this time he had a Chicago Golf Association Handicap of seven. He is in splendid health, has normal blood pressure, and remarkable stamina for a man in his fiftieth year. Unfortunately, a rather remarkable and alarming phenomenon has taken place during the past year. His game deteriorated and he began shooting in the upper nineties. This slump continued and now it is firmly embedded. His smooth and rhythmical swing, once the envy of the entire country club, has changed to a rapid, jerky, unfinished lunge. Added to this, his psychological state has produced a degree of nervousness and irritability that is ruining his reputation and losing him his friends and his clients. When he addresses the ball his large veins stand out from his body, his face flushes, and his jugular vein turns black and pulses violently. Every muscle in his body becomes rigid, and his normally soft features become hard and fierce.

During the past year his handicap, owing to this terrible condition, has gone to 16 and it shows every indication of going even higher. Dr. Golf, unless I can bring him back to his original game and handicap or at least give him back his confidence and his old swing I am afraid he may become physically ill. Two weeks ago, when he had a ninety-nine, I had to restrain him from doing a terrible thing to himself in the shower room.

I am taking the liberty of enclosing my friend's medical and golf histories. I urge you to look into this matter as soon as humanly possible. I am afraid there is nothing else I can do.

Humbly yours,
JACK GELBER, M.D.
Chicago, Ill.

Dr. Gelber,

I have studied your friend and patient's golf and medical histories and I find that you have made an excellent prognosis. It now remains for us to give

this man back his original game. I agree with you
that once we are able to get him back in the low
eighties his nervousness and anxiety will disappear.
He had what appears to be a sound game less than
a year ago, and from your analysis of his golf history
and the photographs I surmise that he had a basically
good swing. I don't like his hip position, but this
is a matter we can take up much later. For the
moment we must strike at the center of his malady
and prevent it from spreading any further.

My first observation is that his current spate of
shanking and skulling (uncontrolled) occurs at the
precise moment of diastolic pulsation. I can see how

you, being a close friend of his, would overlook this coincidence. Possibly his intense coloring and violence concealed this and I am sure that in many cases you simply could not stand the sight and had to turn away. I think we can then safely say that the diastolic is a contributing cause of the violent body pulsation that throws his swing and entire being out of timing and equilibrium. My suggestion, and I feel confident it will work, is to retime his swing with a metronome calibrated to reflect his diastolic-systolic tempo. The swing should then be made to begin at the low period of systolation when the pulse is at the lowest. This is the general treatment I use for high blood pressure patients. The obvious result will be a smooth back swing instead of the jerky pulse-ridden take-a-way he is now experiencing. My logic here is that the heavy diastolic charge causes the violent tremor, which in turn locks the muscles producing the defective swing. This, in turn, feeds back after a heavy secretion of adrenaline to produce an even greater pulsation. We may have to use a few refinements to this treatment so I want you to feel free to wire me after your first meeting with your friend.

The only flaw I can find in your presentation and analysis of this case, which incidentally is not altogether unique, is a rather strange and troublesome tendency to treat physical health and the golf phenomenon as two distinct areas. You are apparently suffering from the old Descartean objective-subjective dualistic logic. I would suggest you reread your Kant and Whitehead on this, and in the future treat physical health and the golf phenomenon not as two distinct provinces, but as the one which they most assuredly are.

As ever,
DR. GOLF

102.

Dear Dr. Golf,

Have you any advice on lining up shots of around 190 to 220 yards? This is one of my most difficult problems.

Regardless of how careful I am in positioning my feet and squaring my shoulders to the hole I always end up with the ball far to the right of where I aim.

PAT JOHNSON
London, England

Dear Sir,

Very few of us indeed have tone-true ears, neither do we have the proper visual balance to insure exact depth perception and measure distances. A navigator does not plunge his ship forward with a mere reading of his compass. He consults his sextant, his chronometer, his charts, and the stars—and then carefully plots his basic course. To this tentative direction he adds or subtracts his magnetic compass variation, and then finally and carefully arrives at what is termed his true heading. Can we not, then, compare the alignment of a long golf shot to this? Are we all not then our own navigators as well as captains?

In my many years of golf I have found that I have a tendency to aim to the right of the hole. On a 250-yard shot this deviation is as much as 7 yards on a windless day. No one told me that my visual variation was 7 yards from this distance. I experimented and found out with various devices and computations what it was, and then made the necessary adjustment.

For the past thirty years I have been marketing, with more than satisfactory success, my Dr. Golf Eagle-Ho directional variation transit. This instrument can be strapped to the bag with far less inconvenience and certainly more practicality than an ordinary umbrella.

Enclosed is a full-color brochure showing this remarkable instrument. The price is $78.68 plus $2.60 postage.

As ever,
Dr. Golf

103.

Dear Dr. Golf,

My problem is back swing. Every article I read discusses back swing in terms of one half, three quarters, etc., but nowhere have I heard what the one half, three quarters, etc., is related to. I realize I am not being clear here. What I mean is precisely what is a proper back swing? How long is it? Can it be measured and does it change with each club?

J. Sheppard
Muscle Shoals, Ala.

Dear Sir,

How well I know your problem. Long have I labored to perfect what I consider the definitive work on back swing. Yes, Mr. Sheppard, there is a full back swing and, what is more, it can now be discussed in terms that can (with a little application) be understood. I am referring to my Eagle-Ho Dr. Golf's *Law of the Back Swing*. This illustrated book with two gate-folded skeletal and anatomical profiles can be obtained for $7.80 plus $2.60 postage. In the book each club is discussed in relation to "The Law." While the *Law of the Back Swing* remains basically constant for all clubs, there are certain refinements and coefficient changes as we progress from the midiron to the niblick and also from the driver to the baffy-spoon. Even the putter back swing can be equated with "The Law."

An example of "The Law" and its usage is on page 987. Following a scrupulous list of precautions that must be observed by persons suffering from an unusual curvature of the spine, abnormal arm length (that length which results in the extended palms falling to or below the patella ligament), excessively stout people, and victims of gigantism, I set down the following paragraph.

The *Law of the Back Swing* states that "a full back swing can be caused by withdrawing the face of the club away from the ball that distance which equals the sum of the following increments: The distance from the center of the person's epistropheus to the lower base of the small coccyx plus the square of the distance from the epistropheus to the topmost portion of the glabella. To this we interpolate our proper height-weight handicap (Eagle-Ho adjusted) coefficient from the proper table and merely multiply this said coefficient to the unresolved figure above. . . ."

All measurements are metric. I strongly suggest one should have a close friend do the actual measuring and also that both parties become thoroughly immersed in the information I have set down on the anatomical and skeletal profiles.

As ever,
Dr. Golf

104.

Dear Dr. Golf,

Three months ago my husband's set of Eagle-Ho woods and irons arrived. Since that time a strange change has come over him. I didn't mind the constant attention and the endless waxing when the clubs first arrived.

As a matter of fact I was actually glad to see that he was getting so much pleasure from them.

But as the days went by and the waxing and the oiling sessions increased I began to worry. I was quiet when he erected a heavy timber across the living room ceiling to hang the clubs from (he claims this keeps them from warping), nor did I say anything when he let the oils and ointments he covered the clubs with drip all over the carpet. But I began to worry when he ripped up the carpeting and replaced it with a thick green brushlike material that simulates an actual green. Eventually I gave over the entire living room to him. I moved the TV set and the big couch into the dining room and allowed him to close the door between us. The first sign of his strangeness came three weeks ago when I discovered he had been locking the door and drawing the blinds.

To this day I do not know what he does in there. But once again I said nothing.

Dr. Golf, the children are in bed now and I am writing from the dining room table under the light from the chandelier. I am desperately in need of help.

Dr. Golf, my husband, a graduate of Princeton and a member of the N. Y. Stock Exchange, has for the past week been taking all of his clubs to bed with him. He places them on the pillow where I once lay. I have taken to sleeping on the couch, for now

there is no room for me. I have kept this awful thing from the children by sending them off to bed early. I am petrified with fear that one of them will walk in and see this awful spectacle. He has been doing this every night for two weeks now. The clubs are placed with the driver nearest him and then the other woods and then the irons. The niblick is on the edge of the pillow. He clutches your Eagle-Ho water-filled-head putter in his left hand.

Dr. Golf, I have no intention of calling the medical men, nor do I wish to lose my husband's love. I have suggested that he go to Pinehurst for a few weeks, but he keeps saying he has too much work to do. I know he is doing no work except rubbing, waxing and oiling his clubs and bag. I am trying to keep calm about this, but I am desperately afraid he may do something foolish on the commuter train or downtown. Dr. Golf, I would like to re-establish our marriage on the basis it was three months ago. I do not want to discourage his golf or his attention to his clubs—I only want the clubs out of the bed and the door to the living room unlocked.

Very truly yours,
MRS. RICHARD KERVAN

Dear Madam,

If my rooms at Eagle-Ho were not all taken I would have your husband out here for a few days. But I don't believe your problem is as serious as you make it sound. Your husband is proud of his set of E-H woods and irons, and he finds it difficult to tear himself away from them. I am glad to hear he is suspending them from the ceiling, for this keeps the hickory shafts straight and supple. In time this intensity will diminish. But you must realize that the intensity is in direct ratio to the enjoyment your husband is experiencing when he gazes upon the superb workmanship and the fine quality of this beautiful set. How well I remember my first set! I don't believe you should discourage your children from seeing this sight. Often a child will prosper from seeing his father in this stage of rapture.

I would say then, take your children by the hand and stand at the foot of the bed while your husband sleeps, and tell these same children what a wonderful man it is that you have married and what a splendid father he is. The children will never forget this and I'm sure that later, after they have grown and got out into the world, it will be one of those little touchstones that do so much to hold families together.

As for advice about getting the clubs out of the bed I would say approach this matter carefully. Your husband is at the absolute peak of enjoyment of his clubs at this time and a sudden rupture might cause irreparable damage. There have been a number of cases like yours in the past and I always give the same advice. In every case the approach has worked and my files are filled with grateful letters from overjoyed wives. My advice is simple and direct: Secure several balls of wool of good quality, making sure the color is of the earth type, i.e., brown, dun, beige, etc.—no reds or pastels or blues. Quickly, but carefully, knit a set of four wood covers. And then some night when your husband is asleep—possibly on his birthday, an anniversary, Christmas or, if possible, Eagle-Ho Day—steal into the chamber and slip each club head cover into place on the respective woods.

Two results will follow. One is the realization that the clubs should have been covered in the night air, and the second is that a labor of love went into the making of the covers. If you can fashion a petit point motif or spell out the names of the clubs in a curling Baroque, the effect will be even more pronounced.

Madam, within the next fortnight you will be writing me again. I am keeping a place in my files open for your letter of appreciation and joy.

As ever,
Dr. Golf

105.

Dear Dr. Golf,

Most of our members of the Ardsley Country Club catch the 4:01 train from Grand Central Station and arrive at the club at 5:06. We change clothes on the train and go directly from the station to the first tee. Our clubs and caddies are ready, and on an average weekday in the summer and the early fall we can get in eighteen holes. But the days grow short when we reach September and we have to play faster and faster to complete the eighteen. By late September we are playing on the dead run. In October we give up on playing eighteen and by cutting across hedgerows and rhododendron and a short skiff ride across the water on the fifteenth we can, on a bright day, get in twelve holes.

Doctor, today is October 27th and the last day of Daylight Saving Time in the East. It is also the day of our annual Deathwatch Tournament. After today there will be no more afternoon golf. Our Deathwatch Tournament today started off in fun, but after the prizes were handed out in the locker room the usual frivolity and towel snapping was replaced by a deep melancholia. Most of the men walked off by themselves, they wanted to be alone, for they know that for them golf is over and only bowling and gin rummy remain until the bright sun of May returns. Dr. Golf, there is no sadder crowd than our members on October 28th, riding the 4:01 and gazing out into the dark night on their northern trip home. Tomorrow is the 28th and I am planning on driving my car to the Van Cortlandt subway stop and taking 'the IND train to town for I cannot bear to see the sad sight of those grim faces pressed against the cold windows of the New York Central coach. I am sure

there is nothing you can do to help me cheer these
souls up, but I thought I would at least ask in the
hope I was overlooking something that could bring
some measure of hope to my sad companions.

Obediently yours,
WILLIAM G. MULLIGAN
Pleasantville, N. Y.

Dear Sir,

The observance of the Standard Time system is
an absurdity. Does a husbandman milk his cows an
hour later on the 28th of October? Does a bird retire
an hour later, a bat an hour earlier on the 28th? And
do the celestial harmonies of the universe pause in
their course for sixty minutes on the 28th day of
October and then proceed? I, sir, say they do not.
Pray tell me, then, why you feel compelled to observe
this custom? Why should the golfers and the hunters
of the world suffer for a system obviously devised
to foster tap dancers and minstrels? I say, turn your
back to this practice and order your caddies to do
the same.

As ever,
DR. GOLF

P.S. It has also come to my attention that there is
an express train that leaves Grand Central Station
at 2:03 and arrives at Ardsley at 2:57.

Adler brüten keine Tauben

Eagles do not give birth to doves